NACUBO

EXCELLENCE IN HIGHER EDUCATION
Guide

BRENT D. RUBEN, PH.D.

An Integrated Approach to Assessment, Planning, and Improvement in Colleges and Universities

Library of Congress Cataloging-in-Publication Data

Ruben, Brent D.
  Excellence in higher education guide : an integrated approach to assessment, planning,
and improvement in colleges and universities / by Brent D. Ruben.
     p. cm.
  Includes bibliographical references and index.
  ISBN 978-1-56972-042-4 (alk. paper) -- ISBN 978-1-56972-041-7 (workbook : alk. paper)
  1. Universities and colleges--Administration. I. Title.
LB2341.R726 2007
378.1'01--dc22
                              2007016465

National Association of College and University Business Officers
Washington, D.C.
www.nacubo.org

Printed in the United States of America

For information on use of *Excellence in Higher Education Guide: An Integrated Approach to Assessment, Planning, and Improvement in Colleges and Universities* program or materials contact Dr. Brent D. Ruben, Executive Director, Center for Organizational Development and Leadership, Rutgers University, 57 U.S. 1, New Brunswick, NJ 08901-8554. Email: ruben@odl.rutgers.edu.

CONTENTS

PREFACE

The *Excellence in Higher Education Guide* integrates two influential approaches to assessment, planning, and improvement. The first is the Baldrige model—that is, the assessment criteria and process used in the Malcolm Baldrige National Quality Award Program, developed and administered by the U.S. National Institute of Standards and Technology. The second is the set of principles employed by the U.S. higher education accrediting associations. The Baldrige model is widely acknowledged as one of the most useful and authoritative organizational assessment models ever developed,[1] and the evaluative frameworks advanced by the accrediting associations are the most visible and broadly applied standards for programmatic and institutional review in U.S. colleges and universities.[2]

The Excellence in Higher Education (EHE) model extends the Baldrige model to address the specific needs of higher education, and it does so in a manner that takes into account the standards and terminology used in accrediting. The result is a new model that benefits from the strengths of the Baldrige Award and accrediting frameworks. Though they often use differing vocabulary, the Baldrige and accrediting models each stress the importance of institutional leadership, assessment, data-based decision making, strategic planning, outcomes measurement, and peer comparisons. They also share the position that review, planning, and continuous improvement are fundamental to institutional effectiveness and should be thoroughly integrated into the fabric of every institution aspiring to excellence. The approaches complement one another in many respects, and together they offer what is perhaps the best available guide to excellence and effectiveness in higher education.

The EHE model can be used by an entire college or university—and by individual administrative, service, and student life organizations, academic departments, and programs within the institution. This cross-cutting capability is an extremely important characteristic of the model. Though assessment typically focuses on the educational activities most directly related to an institution's core mission, all divisions within a college or university are interdependent components of a system and all interact to create the experiences that are the basis for the perceptions—and the reality—of students, visitors, alumni, and the public, as well as faculty and staff. Although distinctions among various functional units of a college or university are meaningful to those of us who work *within* the institution, they are much less distinguishable and less significant to external groups. For our constituencies, what matters is the quality and effectiveness of their overall learning, living, or visiting experience.

The general EHE framework provides an *integrated* approach to assessment, planning, and improvement throughout the institution. The benefits of such an approach include the development of a unifying view of organizational excellence, a collective sense of strengths and priorities for improvement, and a common vocabulary for communicating among faculty and staff across academic, student life, administrative, and service functions.

---

[1] Information on the Baldrige National Quality Program is available at www.quality.nist.gov/.

[2] See the Council for Higher Education Accreditation (www.chea.org/), the Middle States Association of Schools and Colleges (www.msche.org/), the New England Association of Schools and Colleges (www.neasc.org), the North Central Association of Schools and Colleges (www.ncahigherlearningcommission.org), the Northwest Association of Schools and Colleges (www.nwccu.org), the Southern Association of Schools and Colleges (www.sacscoc.org), and the Western Association of Schools and Colleges (www.wascweb.org).

It should be clear from the foregoing comments that this publication and its author owe a debt of gratitude to the Baldrige National Quality Program, the accrediting associations, and all those who have contributed to the publications of those organizations (see "Works Cited and Suggested Readings"). I especially want to extend my personal thanks to Harry Hertz, executive director of the Baldrige National Quality Program; his predecessor, Curt Reimann; Steve Spangehl, director of the North Central Association, Academic Quality Program; Judith Eaton, president of the Council for Higher Education Accreditation; and Jean Avnet Morse, director, and Linda Suskie, executive associate director of the Middle States Commission on Higher Education. All have been generous with their knowledge and insights.

Many thanks to my colleagues at Rutgers who have participated in the Excellence in Higher Education process and who have furthered its evolution. There are now approximately 50 academic, student affairs, service, and administrative departments that have used the model for assessment, planning, and improvement at Rutgers, and much has been learned from each. A number of those units have also participated in research on the impact of the EHE assessment (Ruben et al. 2004; Ruben et al. 2007) and in so doing have made further contributions to the advancement of the program.

I continue to be indebted to colleagues at the roughly 35 other colleges and universities that have used the Excellence in Higher Education framework. Special thanks to Phyllis Hoffman, Ron Coley, and John Cummins at the University of California–Berkeley; Maury Cotter and Kathleen Paris at the University of Wisconsin–Madison; Richard Norman, Willard Haley, and Adolph Haislar at Miami University; Louise Sandmeyer, Ann Dodd, and Carol Everett at Penn State University; John Dew at the University of Alabama; Jim Spring, Molly Nearing, and Christina Knickerbocker at the State University of New York at Binghamton; Jamie Barlowe and Nagi Naganathan at the University of Toledo; and Jill Pollock at Texas A&M University.

A very special note of appreciation to Johnson & Johnson for so generously sharing its knowledge and experience, with particular thanks to Karl Schmidt, Denis Hamilton, Mike Thalacker, Randy Beeman, Donnie Young, Bill Quinn, Bob Bury, Mike Burtha, and Jerry Cianfrocca.

For their enthusiasm about this work and assistance with publication, I want to express my appreciation to the administration and staff at the National Association of College and University Business Officers and, particularly, to Donna Klinger, Connie Adamson, Kathleen Dunn, Susan Jurow, John Walda, and also to Jay Morley. Thanks also to Karen Colburn for her valued assistance with the production of the book.

To my colleagues at the Rutgers Center for Organizational Development and Leadership, I am especially appreciative. This includes Sherrie Tromp, Barbara Corso, Joe Lopez, Kate Immordino, Yana Grushina, and Stacy Smulowitz. Thanks also to Stacey Connaughton, Travis Russ, Lisa Mahajan, Kim Biegel, Jocelyn DeAngelis, Jen Lehr, John Fortunato, and Tricia Nolfi, each of whom has contributed to this project in recent years.

Brent D. Ruben

THE NATIONAL CONTEXT

Higher education institutions contribute immeasurably to the personal and professional lives of students and enrich the intellectual, economic, and cultural fabric of their communities, states, nations, and beyond. Few social institutions have been as highly valued as colleges and universities. For those and other reasons the contributions of the higher education community have been generously acknowleged over the years in popular discourse, and in professional and academic presses.

Despite the traditionally high regard for the work of colleges and universities, we are not insulated from the many contemporary economic, demographic, and policy pressures facing other social institutions. The list of such pressures confronting higher education is a long one, as is underscored in dramatic fashion in the following inventory developed by the Association of American Colleges and Universities (2002, 6–7):

- Changing student demographics

    - Increasing proportion of college graduates as a percentage of the general U.S. population

    - Students lacking recommended college preparatory courses

    - Greater percentage of nontraditional students

- New enrollment patterns

    - Increased part-time enrollment

    - Multiple-institution attendance

    - Distance coursework

- The information explosion

    - Increases in available information

    - Decreased review and quality control of available information

    - Shift from needing to remember facts to finding and evaluating information

    - Increasing need for and importance of lifelong learning

- The technological revolution

    - New types of jobs for graduates

    - Changing nature of the classroom because of technology and online learning

    - Frequent changes in job requirements and the need for continuing education

- Accountability
  - Greater calls for measuring performance
  - More state regulation of the curriculum
  - Concerns about mandated testing
  - Accreditation emphasis on effectiveness and assessment
- New education sites and formats
  - Growth in the for-profit higher education sector
  - Distance education
  - Rise of corporate universities
  - More flexible teaching and learning formats
- The changing nature of the workplace
  - Emphasis on creative problem solving, teamwork, and adaptability
  - Need for high-level intellectual skills
  - Need for employees with greater technological and quantitative literacy
- The global nature of major challenges and opportunities
  - Porosity of national boundaries
  - Increasing international competition for students, faculty, and resources
  - Worldwide environmental impacts
  - Post–September 11, 2001, awareness of global interdependency
- Renewed emphasis on civic responsibility and communal values
  - Rise in student volunteerism
  - Cyclical student activism
  - Increased pressure on colleges and universities to join the community in resolving local problems
- Constraints on resources
  - Increasing competition for scarce resources
  - Decreased state and federal funding
  - Increasing reliance on alternative funding sources
  - Necessity of using existing resources more efficiently

UNDERSTANDING AND RESPONDING CONSTRUCTIVELY TO EXTERNAL CRITIQUE

It seems quite clear that a number of the aforementioned factors will have a significant impact on higher education, and yet as the Association of American Colleges and Universities (2002) notes, the vast majority of them are beyond our control. The good news—if it can be considered such—is that there are other challenges confronting the academic community over which it *is* possible to exercise considerable influence.

Three significant issues that fit this category concern the way we relate to our constituencies, operate our institutions, and deal with changing environmental conditions. These three themes are each important in their own right, and they also connect with a number of other more specific challenges confronting higher education—challenges that highlight the need for systematic review, planning, and innovation.

DEVELOPING NEW STRATEGIES TO MEET INCREASING DEMANDS, OFTEN WITH FEW ADDITIONAL RESOURCES

On campuses across the country, academic, student life, service, and administrative units are being called upon to increase quality, effectiveness, and efficiency in response to internal and external pressures. More often than not, the heightened expectations are accompanied by few, if any, additional resources.

Few good options are available in such situations: ignore the rising expectations, meet the increasing demands by sacrificing quality across the board, look for new approaches to the tasks at hand, or make the hard choice to narrow the scope of activities. Each option carries risks and potential morale problems, and each threatens to compromise the breadth and/or quality of the contribution. A common theme of the strategies that do not include turning a blind eye to heightened service expectations is the need to prioritize the various activities in which an institution, division, or department is engaged. Without a method for prioritizing programs and services, an analysis of their centrality and criticality, and a plan to appropriately match resources to priorities, meaningful decision making and forward movement is extremely difficult.

BRIDGING THE GAP BETWEEN THE ACADEMIC AND ADMINISTRATIVE CULTURES

Faculty members, student affairs professionals, and administrative and support personnel typically have quite different training, roles, and responsibilities. As a consequence, these groups often evolve their own distinctive cultures—cultures that sometimes emphasize the value and achievements of their own members, while failing to recognize and appropriately value the full range of contributions of other groups. Whenever that occurs, a lack of understanding and mutual respect across departmental and faculty-staff lines is a consequence, and that, in turn, undermines effective collaboration, wastes scarce resources, diminishes the effectiveness of programs and services, and undermines the institution's reputation among its constituencies. Heightening the shared understanding of the common challenges that confront higher education in general, and each institution in particular, is an important step to transcending such cultural barriers and promoting more effective collaboration in service to one another and our many constituencies.

THINKING MORE BROADLY ABOUT HIGHER EDUCATION INSTITUTIONS AND DEPARTMENTS AS ORGANIZATIONS

How different are colleges of education, law, communication, liberal arts, and business? How unique are departments of human resources, institutional research, computing services, or admissions? The first list, of course, is composed of academic departments, and the second, of administrative and service units. There are major differences in the content of the programs and services that each type of unit offers. Yet, at a higher level of analysis, all of these units are *organizations* and all operate within a higher education context and, as such, have much in common. To recognize and benefit from those commonalities, we need integrating frameworks and terminology for thinking about, talking about, and analyzing the work of departments and institutions (Massy 2003; Ruben 1995a). Without general frameworks, concepts, and terminology, the sharing of insights, strategies, operational practices, and expertise across departmental boundaries is a formidable challenge.

LEARNING FROM THE EFFECTIVE PRACTICES OF OTHER EDUCATIONAL INSTITUTIONS AND FROM ORGANIZATIONS IN OTHER SECTORS—HEALTH CARE, BUSINESS, AND GOVERNMENT

Barriers to organizational learning occur between higher education and other sectors, as they do between departments and divisions within colleges and universities. In terms of their *academic* mission, colleges and universities are quite unique as institutions. However, many of our administrative, service, and support functions have a number of parallels in health care, government, and business, to which we can compare ourselves, and from which we can learn (Ruben 1995a, 1995b, 2004). It is also the case that some departments in those other sectors engage in research, instruction, and public service or outreach activities that have parallel activities in colleges and universities. To the extent that we are preoccupied by our distinctiveness, we miss the opportunity to learn from the experiences and expertise in other sectors. Equally important is the fact that when we fail to listen effectively and learn from others, our credibility as experts in teaching and learning is compromised, as we are perceived to be failing to adopt the very values and practices we so vigorously advocate for others.

ADOPTING THE PHILOSOPHY OF—AND DAY-TO-DAY COMMITMENT TO—CONTINUOUS IMPROVEMENT

Higher education has long been committed to excellence. However, critics often point out that the pace of change and improvement in colleges and universities is slow—and more episodic than continuous (Spellings 2006a, 2006b). Within higher education, proposed innovations and improvements become the topic of protracted discussion about potential shortcomings, as one alternative model or approach after another is introduced, debated, and discarded. Committees often are formed to investigate the problem in depth and make recommendations, and their recommendations may become input for other committees, which also investigate and make recommendations to still other committees. Sometimes, in the quest for completeness, rigor, and *ideal* solutions, we overlook the less-than-perfect solutions. As a consequence, we may talk ourselves out of making *any* improvements. Or the "window of opportunity" for change may pass before any decisions have been made. Or those involved simply lose the will to invest any more time or energy in the effort. No one would argue that extensive analysis is unimportant to innovation and advancement. Likewise, the alternative of unilateral, top-down decision making is fraught with perils. However, too *much* unfocused analysis and discussion—with no clear plan to move to action—leads to organizational paralysis, and ultimately that is as likely to lead to poor outcomes as is too *little* analysis. Thus, the challenge is to adopt approaches that encourage interaction and consultation but that also ensure that the commitment to timely decision making and change is not simply rhetorical. For our own sake, and to effectively address what is a frequent concern among our critics, greater attention to analysis that results in plans and improvements is important.

EXPANDING THE BASE OF CAPABLE AND COMMITTED LEADERS

To address the many obstacles confronting higher education, strong leadership is needed at all levels in academic, student life, service, and administrative areas. For reasons that are difficult to understand, leadership development has historically not been the priority in higher education that it has been in other sectors (Hecht 2006; Ruben 2004, 2006a; Wolverton and Gmelch 2002). The assumption seems to be that leadership and managerial capabilities will emerge and develop naturally among those who have excelled in academic or technical areas. While that approach does produce some excellent leaders, most would agree that its limitations are readily apparent. The learning curve for new leaders is steep, and the consequences for colleagues and the organization while the necessary learning takes place can be painful. The challenge is to clarify the knowledge and skill bases necessary for effective higher education leadership, and then to create opportunities to attract, develop, and reward people with such capabilities. A vision of what constitutes an effective organization, a commitment to institutional self-reflection, and the competencies necessary to ensure collaborative and continuous improvement are among the key elements needed for the excellence in educational leadership that is so much in demand.

RESPONDING PROACTIVELY TO PRESSURE FOR ACCOUNTABILITY AND OUTCOME MEASUREMENT

Pressure to increase accountability and carefully measure outcomes is increasing at the national, state, and institutional levels (Eaton 2005a; Miller 2006; Schray 2006; Spellings 2006a). There is a growing sentiment that we must develop meaningful criteria for assessing the quality and effectiveness of our institutions and our academic, student life, administrative, and service programs and services, as well as criteria to measure and track organizational achievements and outcomes. The resulting information can be used to compare our work to that of peer institutions with whom we share a similar mission, as well as to inform decision making and resource allocation. If we are proactive, pressure for assessment can also be an opportunity: who would disagree with the assertion that it is essential to determine, document, and ensure the quality of our work? In the spirit of review and evaluation that are central to so much of the work of the academy, it can certainly be beneficial to direct some of our analytic energies inward to look more systematically at our own activities and their consequences. Moreover, too much recalcitrance or delay in addressing these issues is likely to result in assessment criteria and processes being defined and imposed by others. The result is likely to be much less satisfying and helpful than if the higher education community takes the leadership role with regard to meaningful outcome assessment.

ADOPTING A BROADER VISION OF EXCELLENCE

Colleges and universities have a long-standing tradition of quality in academics and scholarship. In this respect, higher education is the gold standard—the model to which other sectors look for excellence. But increasingly today there are competing views as to what constitutes excellence in higher education. At least three quite different points of view are evident (Volkwein 2006). First, there is what might be termed the *resource/reputational perspective*, which emphasizes the importance of institutional and disciplinary ratings and rankings, faculty accomplishments and credentials, available financial and material resources, student ranks and test scores, levels of research, and donor funding. The *client-centered model*, which provides a second point of view, focuses on the student experience, the quality of educational practice, program and faculty availability, tuition levels, access, alumni and employer views, and most especially student satisfaction with programs, services, and facilities. The third model, the *strategic investment model*, focuses on return on investment, cost-benefit analysis, control of expenditures, regulation and compliance, and productivity measures including admission yield, retention, time to degree, and expenditure per student (Volkwein 2006). The first of these models tends to be the preferred model of many faculty and has been traditionally important for external reviews, including accreditations, although this pattern is changing. Students, parents, alumni, and employers often emphasize the second, client-centered model. Government officials, boards, and trustees are generally drawn to the perspective of the strategic investment model.

University administrators struggle to reconcile these approaches, recognizing the implications of all three (Volkwein 2006). Each perspective has value, and they are not mutually exclusive. In fact, it seems likely that the most successful institutions, departments, and programs will find ways to embrace all three. Certainly it makes sense to aspire to high standards in student, faculty, programmatic, departmental/disciplinary, and institutional ranking; in our relations with our constituencies; and also in the strategic use of resources and return on investment. To be successful in pursuing these goals, we need to formulate and adopt a broader, more inclusive understanding of excellence—one that leads us to aspire to excellence in all that we do (Ruben 2004).

INTEGRATING APPROACHES TO ASSESSMENT, PLANNING, AND CONTINUOUS IMPROVEMENT

Most colleges and universities have procedures for conducting academic review, planning, and improvement. Within many institutions, however, such activities may be administered in different offices and the functions may not be well integrated. For example, the evaluation and planning activities that occur at the institutional level may not be clearly linked to those undertaken at the program or department level. Or the standards and approaches used in administrative and service areas may differ from those used in academic or student life areas. Most colleges and universities would benefit from having a unifying framework and common language to guide review, planning, and improvement at all levels and across various departments and programs. Among other benefits, a unified model of this kind would promote the exchange of good ideas and increase the adoption of effective practices throughout an institution.

AN INTEGRATED APPROACH TO ASSESSMENT, PLANNING, CONTINUOUS IMPROVEMENT, AND LEADERSHIP

Excellence in Higher Education: An Integrated Approach to Assessment, Planning, and Improvement in Colleges and Universities is designed to help address many of the challenges confronting higher education—particularly those over which we can exercise some direct influence.

The goal of this publication is to offer a comprehensive guide to the processes of review, planning, and continuous improvement for academic, student affairs, administrative, and service units within a college or university—and to do so by adapting the Baldrige framework to higher education in a way that takes account of accrediting standards and terminology.

ACCREDITATION

Historically, accreditation has been the most visible influence for reflective review within higher education. Through a process that includes self-study and peer review, the professional, special focus, and regional accrediting agencies provide a regularized, structured mechanism for quality assurance and improvement for the U.S. higher education community (Eaton 2006). The Council for Higher Education Accreditation (CHEA) has more than 80 accrediting member organizations that oversee the review and accreditation for some 7,000 institutions and 17,000 programs (CHEA 2007; Eaton 2006).

Although some have suggested that accrediting could benefit from increased transparency and national standardization (Schray 2006; Spellings 2006a, 2006b), there is no question that the regional accrediting associations—as well as the professional and other associations—have long been a driving force in promoting increased attention to assessment, planning, and continuous improvement through their standards and guidelines (CHEA 2007; Eaton 2006; Middle States Commission 2002, 2006; New England Association 2004; North Central Association 2007; Northwest Commission 2004; Southern Association 2003; Spangehl 2000, 2004; Western Association 2002).

The description provided by the Western Association of Schools and Colleges is quite typical in this regard: one of the primary goals of accreditation is "promoting within institutions a culture of evidence where indicators of performance are regularly developed and data collected to inform institutional decision making, planning, and improvement" (2002, 6).

Traditionally, the academic mission and programs of colleges and universities provided the primary focus for institutional accreditation. In the current environment, given the broad challenges confronting higher education, national, state, and institutional pressures for fiscal constraint, accountability, attention to learning outcomes assessment, productivity measurement, mission clarity and distinctiveness, and institutional structure all converge in the accrediting process.

Current accreditation standards and practices give increasing attention to *measurement and outcomes* and focus less on *intentions and inputs*. Underpinning this shift is an expanded focus on the received experience of students as distinct from institutional intentions, structures, expertise, and plans of faculty and staff (Ruben 2007). Greater emphasis is also being given to assessing the effectiveness of the institution or program, holistically, as an *organization*. Moreover, accrediting processes are focusing more on student learning and the "value added" by the teaching/learning experience (and for residential colleges and universities, the living experience) provided by the institution. It is worth mentioning that the growing interest in assessment is not unique to higher education; the trend toward giving greater emphasis to measuring performance in terms of outputs and value added has become pervasive in business, health care, and government, as well (Brancato 1995; Kaplan and Norton 1992, 1993, 1996, 2001; Ruben 2004).

Accreditation emphasizes programmatic and institutional self-examination and peer review, and the higher education community has always been a primary audience for the process and its results. With growing concerns about accountability, value, access, and transparency, accreditation has come to serve an increasingly significant "gatekeeper" function for external constituencies, including federal and state governments and the general public. As CHEA president Judith Eaton notes, "Accreditation [now] has many masters and mistresses" (Eaton 2005a). As articulated by one of the regional associations, the accreditation process "stimulates evaluation and improvement, while providing a means of continuing accountability to constituents and the public" (Southern Association 2006, 4).

As accreditation has evolved to serve a broader array of stakeholders and functions, there has been an understandable concomitant shift toward increasingly systemic reviews of institutions and programs. This broadened perspective acknowledges the contribution of all component units and functions—academic, but also student affairs, services, and administration—to the overall success of a program or institution. There may have been a time, for example, when the excellence of institutions or programs was understood to be a natural and inevitable consequence of assembling distinguished faculty members. Today, however, a more multifaceted and nuanced perspective is increasingly required, as it has become apparent that institutional or programmatic excellence is contingent on many factors beyond the excellence of individual faculty members.

THE BALDRIGE FRAMEWORK

Of the various rigorous and systemic approaches to the assessment, planning, and improvement of organizations, none has been more successful or more influential than the Malcolm Baldrige model (Baldrige 2006). The U.S. Congress established the Malcolm Baldrige National Quality Award Program in 1987. Named after Malcolm Baldrige, who served as secretary of commerce from 1981 until his death in 1987, the intent of the program is to promote U.S. business effectiveness for the advancement of the national economy by providing a systems approach to organizational assessment and improvement. More specifically, the goals of the program are as follows:

- Identify the essential components of organizational excellence.
- Recognize organizations that demonstrate those characteristics.
- Promote information sharing by exemplary organizations.
- Encourage the adoption of effective organizational principles and practices.

The program, which is administered by the National Institute of Standards and Technology, has been extremely important in national and international efforts to identify and encourage the application of core principles of organizational excellence. Some 50 state, local, and regional award programs have been created based on Baldrige (Calhoun 2002; Vokurka 2001), and more than 25 different countries have used the Baldrige criteria as the basis for their own national awards that have Baldrige concepts as their foundation (Przasnyski and Tai 2002). In total, there are approximately 60 national awards in other countries (Vokurka 2001).

ACCREDITATION AND BALDRIGE: COMPLEMENTARY APPROACHES

The Baldrige principles and the standards of the accrediting associations have been extremely influential in their respective spheres, and there is a natural and growing compatibility between them (Baldrige 2007a, 2007b; Baenninger and Morse 2004; Driscoll and Cordero de Noriega 2006; Middle States Commission 2006; Nelser 2004; New England Association 2004; North Central Association 2003, 2007; Northwest Commission 2004; Ruben 2004, 2005a, 2005b, 2007; Southern Association 2006, 2003; Spangehl 2000, 2004; Western Association 2002).

Generally speaking, to be valid and useful, any higher education assessment model must have four characteristics. It should provide: 1) a framework that articulates relevant standards for the purposes at hand; 2) detailed descriptions and operationalizations of these standards; 3) methods that allow the standards to be consistently applied by different individuals and in varying institutional settings; and 4) results that are useful for evaluation and improvement within and across institutions.

The approaches of regional, professional, and other accrediting agencies exemplify these characteristics. Though differing somewhat from agency to agency, the models provide a comprehensive set of standards for evaluating quality that are intended to be sufficiently flexible to be useful in reviewing a variety of institutional types with varying missions, and yet are also sufficiently generic to permit broad comparisons among these institutions. These accrediting frameworks provide clear and reasonably precise descriptions of these standards and have various guidelines and training methods in place that are designed to assure that these descriptions will be reliable and applied in a consistent manner. Additionally, the end product of the assessments are designed to be useful for evaluative and improvement purposes.

Baldrige provides yet another such framework, rubric, or model. While "Baldrige" is perhaps best known as an awards or recognition program, it is more fundamentally a way of thinking, a philosophy, and a methodology for conceptualizing, operationalizing, and assessing organizational excellence. The framework provided by the Baldrige, and Baldrige-based programs like *Excellence in Higher Education*, identifies standards considered to be critical to organizational **effectiveness** and quality. Typically, these models include seven broad categories with subcategories, each of which includes precise descriptions of issues and themes to guide the operationalization of the criteria. As with the standards of the accrediting agencies, those of the Baldrige are sufficiently generic to allow useful analyses across varying types of institutions and missions. They are also sufficiently precise so as to provide a useful operational guide to excellence and improvement within specific institutions. Because of their flexibility and generic character, Baldrige-based models can be used not only in the review of entire institutions, but also in the assessment and analysis of individual departments within any such institution.

In each Baldrige-based assessment, the first step is a careful consideration of the institution or department's mission, followed by an examination of issues related to quality and alignment of the organization's plans, goals, leadership practices, programs and services; stakeholder expectations and needs; workplace and workforce profile; assessment systems; and evidence of results. Baldrige-based models typically incorporate a rigorous methodology and extensive annual multi-day training sessions for examiners to facilitate the consistent application of these standards across individuals, institutions, and settings. Typically, Baldrige assessment also includes quantitative as well as qualitative ratings by examiners for each of the standards. The goal is to provide precise documentation as to the level of accomplishment, maturity, or compliance, and also to provide a baseline for comparisons over time and with other organizations. An additional attribute of Baldrige-based models is that they embody a set of standards and a rubric that has been found to be useful in healthcare, government, and business institutions of varying sizes and complexity, as well as in higher education, and as a consequence, are useful for encouraging cross-sector communication and the sharing of relevant effective practices.

The accreditation process "stimulates evaluation and improvement, while providing a means of continuing accountability to constituents and the public" (Southern Association 2004, 3). The same can be said of the Baldrige approach. Each emphasizes the importance of broadly defining excellence; valuing leadership and planning; establishing clear, shared, and measurable goals; creating effective programs and departments; conducting systematic assessments of outcomes; and engaging in comparisons with peers and leaders.[1] At their core, the two frameworks have a great deal in common. Both reflect a commitment to an iterative process of mission-based goal setting, assessment, and improvement, as illustrated in Figure 1.

In addition to integrating concepts from the Baldrige and accreditation approaches, the Excellence in Higher Education framework integrates elements from management audits, disciplinary reviews, and strategic planning to provide a generic model broadly applicable across all functions and levels of an institution. (See Figure 2.)

FIGURE 1: CORE PRINCIPLES OF BALDRIGE-BASED AND ACCREDITATION FRAMEWORKS

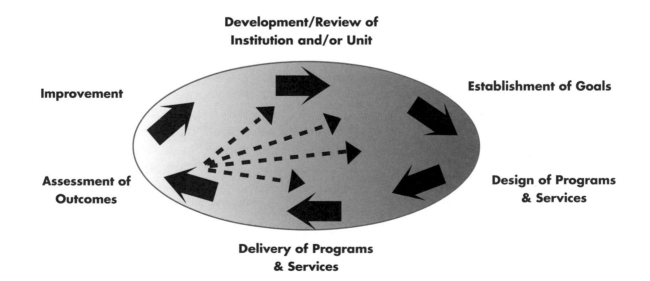

EXCELLENCE IN HIGHER EDUCATION

FIGURE 2: HIGHER EDUCATION REVIEW AND IMPROVEMENT APPROACHES

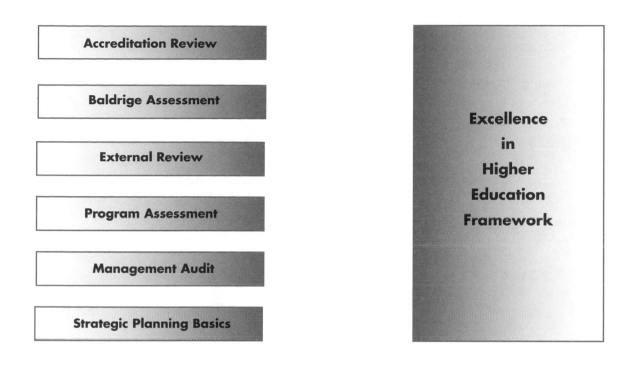

The framework is appropriate for use by administrative, service, student affairs, or academic units and by programs, centers, or institutes. Moreover, the guidelines can be used by an entire college or university or by a group such as a program faculty, an administrative assembly, an advisory board, or a senate. Having a common model adaptable for use in so many diverse ways throughout the institution can be extremely helpful in promoting a shared vision and unifying standards of excellence. Moreover, EHE facilitates communication and the sharing of effective-practice approaches, outcomes that, in turn, increase the possibility of ongoing collaboration between and among departments and programs.

USES OF THE EXCELLENCE IN HIGHER EDUCATION FRAMEWORK

GUIDE FOR SELF-ASSESSMENT, PLANNING, AND IMPROVEMENT

The EHE program's most common application is as a guide for institutional or departmental self-assessment or as a resource to institute an integrated program of assessment, planning, and continuous improvement. When used for either purpose, a seminar, workshop, or retreat is generally the format used to introduce the program. This book and its companion publications, the *Workbook and Scoring Instructions* and the *Facilitator's Guide*, provide information, explanatory materials, and a supporting PowerPoint presentation for those who wish to use the EHE framework as the basis for workshops or seminars. They also include instructions on Baldrige-based scoring for those who wish to employ a quantitative approach in their review.

One can also use this guide as a source for the standards to apply in an external or peer review of an academic, student life, administrative, or service unit—or a college or university as a whole. Or the EHE framework can be utilized as a foundation for an accreditation self-study process. Yet another alternative is to use the EHE guide and supplementary publications in preparing for a Baldrige award application—either for a national award or for consideration by one of the many state quality programs that mirror Baldrige.

A LEADER'S GUIDE

The Excellence in Higher Education model offers both theoretical and practical guidance for leaders and planners at all levels in a college or university (Ruben 2006a). Although EHE is not intended to be a how-to guide for strategic planning or leadership (for other sources that do offer such guidance, see the "Works Cited and Suggested Readings" at the end of this book), it does offer a systemic and integrated vision of organizational excellence and a "checklist" of key areas to be considered in determining where an institution, department, or program stands in relation to that vision. In so doing, it establishes the kind of foundation that is essential for effective leadership. The guide is helpful in this regard, as is the workbook, which includes summary outlines of each category presented in a checklist format.

Regardless of the specific application made of the EHE framework, it has a number of benefits (Ruben et al. 2004; Ruben et al. 2007):

- Provides a standard of comparison and baseline measures using an accepted organizational assessment framework

- Sharpens the focus on the needs, expectations, perspectives, experiences, and satisfaction/dissatisfaction levels of the groups served by an institution's or department's activities, programs, or services

- Provides a vocabulary and shared framework for organizational analysis and improvement that uses the language of higher education

- Highlights and clarifies organizational strengths

- Identifies and prioritizes potential areas for improvement

- Facilitates communication and constructive comparisons within and across units and institutions

- Broadens faculty and staff participation in organizational review and strategic planning

- Provides a proactive and constructive response to demands for increased assessment, accountability, and outcome measurement

- Offers a framework to guide leaders

- Provides a useful foundation for accreditation linked to continuous improvement

NOTE

1. For a comparative analysis of educational goals and outcomes identified by the regional and professional accrediting associations, see Association of American Colleges and Universities (2004, 20–21).

THE FRAMEWORK AND REVIEW PROCESS

CORE CONCEPTS AND VALUES

The Excellence in Higher Education framework and process focus on elements essential to establishing and maintaining an outstanding institution, department, or program. The framework is built around the following core concepts and values:

- *A clear sense of purpose (mission) and future aspirations (vision)* broadly shared, understood, and valued

- *Effective leadership and governance processes* at all levels, including mechanisms for feedback and review

- *Strategic planning, plans, priorities, and goals* to translate purposes and aspirations into specific programs, services, and activities and to ensure that operations and resources are effectively and efficiently used in support of such directions

- *High-quality programs and services,* consistent with the established mission and aspirations, carefully designed, regularly evaluated, and continuously improved

- *Strong and mutually valued relationships* with constituencies, particularly with those individuals and groups who benefit most directly from the programs and services offered by the institution or department

- *Information about the needs, expectations, and experiences of key constituencies,* gathered and used as inputs to program and service development, review, and improvement and to guide day-to-day decision making and resource allocation

- *Qualified and dedicated faculty and staff and a satisfying work environment,* with ongoing review and improvement as priorities

- *Systematic review processes* and the *assessment of outcomes* to determine how successfully the institution, department, or program is fulfilling its mission, aspirations, and goals; to document current strengths; and to identify improvement priorities

- *Comparisons with peers and leaders* to encourage innovation and improvement and to provide a context for clarifying strengths and areas in need of improvement

The EHE framework is built on the assumption that whatever the nature of the system, institution, division, department, or program, the foregoing concepts are equally appropriate as criteria for assessment, planning, and improvement, and equally useful as guides for leaders.

FIGURE 3. EXCELLENCE IN HIGHER EDUCATION FRAMEWORK

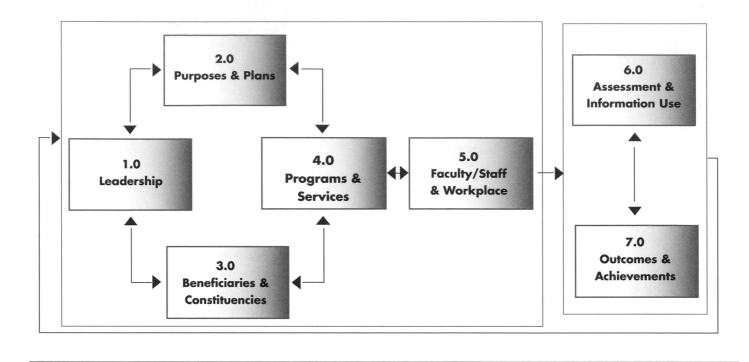

Structurally, the EHE framework, illustrated in Figure 3, is composed of questions grouped into seven major categories:[1]

1. Leadership
2. Purposes and plans
3. Beneficiaries and constituencies
4. Programs and services
5. Faculty/staff and workplace
6. Assessment and information use
7. Outcomes and achievements

EHE provides a structured guide for reviewing each of these areas as they operate within a particular institution, department, or program. Categories 1–5 are fundamental building blocks in any effective organization, Category 6 focuses on methods and procedures in place to assess quality and effectiveness in each of these five areas. Category 7 considers the outcomes and achievements that are documented through the assessment process. Knowledge derived from assessment and outcomes (categories 6 and 7) is important in its own right, but also, as Figure 3 shows, provides vital input for leadership, planning, programs and services, and faculty/staff and workplace enhancement. It is this feedback loop that is so critical to continuous improvement. Together, working in interaction, these components constitute a system that is the essence of an academic, student life, service, or administrative unit—and of a college or institution as a whole.

THE REVIEW PROCESS

The EHE process consists of a category-by-category review of each of the seven major areas. Essentially, the review "freezes" the ongoing dynamics of an organization, focusing on each component individually to provide a clear picture of the strengths and potential areas for improvement of the unit or institution in that area.

The review process for categories 1 through 6 considers *approach and implementation*. *Approach* refers to the methods and strategies used. *Implementation* refers to the manner and extent to which approaches are applied and enacted within an organization. Key questions for these categories, therefore, relate to how the institution or department approaches and implements activities in the areas of leadership, planning, relations with beneficiaries and constituencies, programs and services, faculty/staff and the workplace, and assessment. The focus of Category 7 is on results. The term *results* refers to documented evidence of outcomes, accomplishments, and achievements, and therefore, questions in this category relate to documented results for each of the previous categories.

NOTE

1. The EHE and Baldrige models differ somewhat in the terminology used and concepts emphasized, as well as in the sequence of categories. Organizationally, the major differences are that EHE addresses assessment and information-sharing issues in Category 6, whereas the Baldrige framework considers those concepts in Category 4. See http://baldrige.nist.gov/Criteria.htm.

COMPONENTS OF THE EXCELLENCE IN HIGHER EDUCATION MODEL

THE CATEGORIES AND ASSOCIATED CONCEPTS

THE OVERVIEW: ESTABLISHING THE CONTEXT

In the EHE framework, an overview section precedes the seven categories. The overview consists of questions designed to garner a general description of the institution, department, or program—its structure, key constituencies, and other characteristics—as noted in the outline in Figure 4.

CATEGORY 1: LEADERSHIP

Category 1 is concerned with leadership approaches and governance systems used to guide the institution, department, or program. It looks at how leaders and leadership practices encourage excellence, effectiveness, engagement, innovation, and attention to the needs of individuals, groups, and/or organizations that benefit from programs and services and how leadership practices are reviewed and improved upon.

CATEGORY 2: PURPOSES AND PLANS

The purposes and plans category focuses on organizational directions, aspirations, and plans. It begins by looking at how the institution, department, or program reviews, refines, and/or reaffirms its mission, vision, and broad organizational goals; it then considers how such organizational directions are translated into priorities and action steps and then implemented. The category also looks at how faculty and staff are engaged in these activities.

CATEGORY 3: BENEFICIARIES AND CONSTITUENCIES

The beneficiaries and constituencies category focuses on the groups that benefit from—or otherwise influence or are influenced by—the programs and services offered by the institution, department, or program being reviewed. The category asks how the organization learns about the needs, perceptions, and priorities of those groups, and how that information is used to enhance the unit's working relationships with those constituencies.

CATEGORY 4: PROGRAMS AND SERVICES

Category 4 focuses on the mission-critical programs and services the institution, department, or program offers, and on how quality and effectiveness are ensured. Consideration is also given to important operational and support services.

CATEGORY 5: FACULTY/STAFF AND WORKPLACE

Category 5 considers how the institution, department, or program being reviewed recruits and retains faculty and staff, encourages excellence and engagement, creates and maintains a positive workplace culture and climate, and promotes and facilitates personal and professional development.

CATEGORY 6: ASSESSMENT AND INFORMATION USE

Category 6 focuses on the approach used by the institution, department, or program to review and monitor progress relative to its purposes and plans, leadership effectiveness, relations with beneficiaries and constituencies, programs and services quality, faculty/staff relations and workplace climate, and assessment processes. This category also considers how the organization maintains its internal assessment and peer review system and how it uses both for continuous improvement.

CATEGORY 7: OUTCOMES AND ACHIEVEMENTS

Reporting outcomes and achievements is the theme of Category 7. The category asks for information and evidence to document or demonstrate the quality and effectiveness of the institution, department, or program, trends over time, and the unit's standing in comparison with peers and leaders in the field.

FIGURE 4. CATEGORIES AND ITEMS

Institution, Department, or Program Overview

0.1 Mission, structure, and personnel
0.2 Programs, services, and constituencies
0.3 Peers and comparisons
0.4 Challenges and opportunities

1.0 Leadership

1.1 Organizational leadership
1.2 Public and professional leadership
1.3 Ethics and social responsibility

2.0 Purposes and Plans

2.1 Plan development
2.2 Plan implementation

3.0 Beneficiaries and Constituencies

3.1 Needs and expectations
3.2 Relationship enhancement

4.0 Programs and Services

4.1 Mission-critical programs, services, and processes
4.2 Operational and support services and processes

5.0 Faculty, Staff, and Workplace

5.1 Faculty and staff
5.2 Workplace

6.0 Assessment and Information Use

6.1 Assessment approach and methods
6.2 Comparative analysis
6.3 Information sharing and use

7.0 Outcomes and Achievements

7.1 Leadership
7.2 Purposes and plans
7.3 Beneficiaries and constituency groups
7.4 Mission-critical programs, services, and processes
7.5 Operational and support services and processes
7.6 Faculty, staff, and workplace
7.7 Assessment and information sharing

OVERVIEW OF THE INSTITUTION, DEPARTMENT, OR PROGRAM

Meaningful assessment begins with a high-level description, or overview, of the institution, department, or program and the context in which it operates. The overview includes descriptions of mission, structure, personnel, major programs and services, and key constituencies. The following are integral as well: a listing of peers and competitors, leaders in the field, major recommendations from previous internal or external assessments, and key challenges and opportunities facing the organization.

Assembling and formatting this information into a brief summary document is a very useful exercise as a part of the preparation for a review. The resulting overview is a helpful background document for the organization itself, for individuals outside the organization who may be participating in the review, and for those who will be interested in the final outcomes of the review process.

0.1. MISSION, STRUCTURE, AND PERSONNEL

Briefly describe the institution, department, or program that will be the focus of the assessment, including the following:

1. What is the name of the organization,[1] and what is its primary purpose or mission?

2. How is the organization structured?

3. What are the key elements of the leadership and governance structure?

4. Who are the senior leaders, and what are their primary areas of responsibility?

5. To whom does the senior leader of the organization report?

6. Does the institution, department, or program have advisory or governing boards, and if so, what are their roles and responsibilities?

7. How many full- and part-time faculty and/or staff work in the institution, department, or program? Briefly describe the responsibilities of each employee group. Which groups are unionized?

8. What are the major facilities, equipment, and technologies for which the organization has responsibility?

9. What is the legal, regulatory, licensing, and/or accrediting environment in which the institution, department, or program operates? Briefly describe any mandated standards, review processes, and financial or environmental regulations that may apply.

10. Has the institution, department, or program participated in self-assessments, external assessments, or other reviews within the past five years? What were the major conclusions and recommendations, and what, if any, actions have been undertaken in response to those assessments?

0.2. PROGRAMS, SERVICES, AND CONSTITUENCIES[2]

1. What are the major programs and/or services provided by the institution, department, or program?

2. For what beneficiary groups does the institution, department, or program provide its programs and services? What is the approximate size of each of those groups, and in general terms, what are their expectations and/or requirements?

3. With what other organizations does the unit have formalized collaborative relationships, alliances, or partnerships? Briefly describe the nature and purposes of each. Also, list and describe any key informal relationships with external groups or organizations. List other institutions or units with which the institution, department, or program interacts on a regular basis.

0.3. PEERS, COMPETITORS, AND LEADERS

1. What institutions, departments, or programs are considered to be peers, competitors, and leaders in the field or discipline?

2. In terms of overall quality, stature, or standing, how does the institution, department, or program being reviewed compare with peers, competitors, or leaders?

3. What are the principal factors that influence the institution's, department's, or program's success and standing relative to others in the field?

0.4. CHALLENGES AND OPPORTUNITIES

1. What are the most critical organizational challenges at this time?

2. What special opportunities exist for advancing the quality, stature, or standing of the organization?

NOTES

1. The terms *organization* and *unit* are used in a general sense to refer to an entire institution; an administrative, service, student service, or academic department, program, center, or institute; or an administrative group, assembly, or senate.

2. The term *constituency* refers to any stakeholder group or organization that is important to the work of an institution, department, or program—because it benefits from, influences, or is influenced by the organization. Thus, it applies to advisory or regulatory boards, other departments that provide resources, and units with which your organization collaborates. Similarly, while members of the senior administration might not be considered beneficiaries of the work of your organization in the most precise sense of the term, they would certainly constitute an important constituency group.

1.0

LEADERSHIP

Few concepts are as widely discussed in the literature of organizations as leadership. Although perspectives on the topic differ considerably from one author to another, there is widespread agreement that leadership is the cornerstone of excellence in any organization. In the context of higher education, the primary function of leadership and governance is, in the words of the Middle States Commission, to help an organization "realize fully its stated mission and goals and to achieve these in the most effective and efficient manner.... Institutional governance provides the means through which authority and responsibility are assigned, delegated, and shared in a climate of mutual support" (Middle States Commission 2006, 12).

Senior leaders and others involved in institutional governance have the responsibility of guiding the institution, department, or program in the pursuit of a clear and shared sense of purpose and direction, facilitating the development and implementation of goals and plans, establishing a culture of collaboration and collegiality, inspiring high standards of quality and productivity, encouraging civic and ethical responsibility, and promoting and modeling these desired organizational outcomes and values through their own behavior.

Additionally, exemplary leadership involves a commitment to the sharing of expertise and experience beyond the boundaries of the organization through contributions to campus, public, and professional communities. Also important is a dedication to high standards of integrity, ethical conduct, and social responsibility to ensure that "the institution adheres to the highest ethical standards in its representation to its constituencies and the public; in its teaching, scholarship, and service; in its treatment of its students, faculty, and staff; and its relationships with regulatory and accrediting agencies" (Northwest Commission 2004, 1, standard 9).

Although such responsibilities are central to the duties of senior leaders, almost all leaders in all areas and at all levels share them.

CHALLENGES OF HIGHER EDUCATION LEADERSHIP

The difficulties facing higher education leaders are arguably among the most daunting anywhere. Individuals in leadership roles in colleges and universities must take account of national challenges, local and institutional goals and priorities, a diverse and often seemingly irreconcilable array of stakeholder expectations, and the demands of bright and independent colleagues. They typically have limited resources, and they often have few incentives to encourage new initiatives or foster significant change or renewal.

Another significant challenge—particularly as it relates to academic leadership—lies in the fact that those who come to leadership and governance positions from faculty or professional positions have often had little formalized preparation for those roles as part of their education (Gmelch 2000; Hecht 2006; Ruben 2004, 2006a; Wolverton and Gmelch 2002). Graduate education encourages independent thinking and problem solving and places great value on having the answers and being able to articulate and defend one's viewpoint effectively—indispensable skills for guiding one's own professional career. However, an organizational leader needs other talents: skill in creating consensus on priorities; facility for consultation in thought and action; and the ability to defer or sublimate one's own point of view. In such roles, facilitating and coordinating the contributions of others is critical, as is becoming a student of organizational politics and the economics of higher education. A successful leader must learn to focus his or her primary efforts on promoting the personal and professional recognition of others' accomplishments and careers—and the achievements of the department or institution—more than on his or her own achievements.

How these challenging tasks can be accomplished effectively—and how people with these capabilities can best be identified, developed, and appropriately rewarded—is a matter of continuing discussion and the topic of many writings on the subject of leadership in higher education (e.g., Gempesaw 2004; Morley 2004; Ruben 2006b; Warzynski and Chabot 2004; Willits and Pollack 2004).

DIMENSIONS OF LEADERSHIP EXCELLENCE

Judging from the evidence, there is no simple formula for achieving excellence in higher education leadership, but a number of critical dimensions can be listed:

- Having a well-defined and inclusive view of organizational excellence, and the competencies required for its realization
- Creating a shared commitment to the organization's purposes, needs, and aspirations and maintaining a focus on strategic goals and directions to achieve those ends
- Learning about and educating colleagues about opportunities and political and economic challenges facing higher education in general, and the institution, department, or program more specifically
- Being a strong advocate for listening carefully to the voices of individuals, groups, and organizations who are the potential beneficiaries of the work of the institution, department, or program, and encouraging colleagues to do likewise
- Fostering a culture wherein ongoing assessment and improvement as well as fact-based decision making, resource allocation, and planning are accepted practices
- Developing an integrated system of leadership and governance to encourage effective and coordinated leadership throughout the organization
- Fostering accountability through the establishment of clear goals and the systematic assessment of outcomes
- Encouraging and using feedback on leadership and institutional effectiveness
- Engaging and motivating colleagues at all levels to contribute to the best of their capabilities
- Promoting teamwork, collaborative problem solving, and a sense of community
- Encouraging leadership and professional development and recognizing the values of personal and organizational learning

- Viewing change as a positive and necessary component of organizational excellence
- Effectively representing the program, department, and/or institution with external groups and organizations
- Maintaining and promoting high standards of integrity and ethical and social responsibility

One of the most fundamental tenets of leadership practice is that leaders are most effective when they are personally and visibly engaged in their work in a manner that demonstrates their commitment to the organizational values and principles, through their actions as well as through their words. Through their behavior, leaders have the opportunity to reaffirm and reinforce the importance of listening to and understanding the perspectives of those served by the organization, engaging and valuing colleagues at all levels, promoting an open and constructive exchange of viewpoints, and encouraging collaborative leadership and accountability throughout the organization. Personal involvement, communication, and consensus building are important in *all* organizations; in higher education they are particularly crucial because of the range of challenges that must be addressed, the traditions of shared governance, and the limited number of incentives and rewards that most leaders have available to encourage change.

1.0. LEADERSHIP: KEY REVIEW ISSUES

Category 1 of the review focuses on how leaders and leadership practices guide the organization in clarifying and sustaining consensus on its purposes and future directions; how they promote a focus on the needs and expectations of key constituencies;[1] and how they establish a culture of collaboration and collegiality in planning and decision making. Also examined are how the leadership approaches foster effective, engaged, and consultative leadership and governance throughout the organization[2] and how leadership effectiveness is assessed. Finally, the category focuses on the ways in which leaders share their own and the organization's experience and expertise with campus, public, and professional groups and how high standards of ethical and social responsibility are established and maintained.

1.1. ORGANIZATIONAL LEADERSHIP

AREAS TO ADDRESS

A. Leadership and Governance Structure and Practice
  1. **What is the leadership and governance structure of the organization?**

- What are the formal reporting relationships within the institution, department, or program?
- What are the areas of responsibility of those in leadership positions?
- How are those in leadership positions chosen, and what criteria guide the selection process?
- At whose pleasure, and for how long, do leaders serve?
- Are leadership and governance roles, responsibilities, and reporting relationships well documented?
- How is information regarding leadership and governance roles, responsibilities, and reporting relationships disseminated?[3]

2. **How do leadership practices clarify and advance the organization's mission, aspirations, and goals?**

- How are leaders personally and visibly involved in promoting the directions, aspirations, and values of the program, department, and/or institution?

- What leadership approaches are employed to develop shared understanding of established organizational purposes, directions, aspirations, and goals among colleagues and external constituencies?

- How do senior leaders engage others throughout the organization in the periodic assessment and review of the institution's stated mission, aspirations, and goals?

3. **What personal roles and responsibilities do leaders at various levels have relative to:**
- Clarifying purposes and aspirations?
- Strategic planning?
- Resource allocation?
- Internal communication?
- External relations and public communication?
- Encouraging assessment and the use of outcomes information for improvement?

4. **What role do senior leaders play in fostering an organizational culture and climate that:**
- Promotes high standards of individual and collective achievement?
- Values assessment, planning, and improvement?
- Uses data and information to guide decision making and problem solving?
- Encourages initiative and innovation?
- Advances personal and organizational learning?
- Fosters organizational flexibility and agility?
- Encourages collaboration and teamwork?
- Values outreach, service, and responsiveness to the needs and expectations of groups and organizations for which programs or services are provided?

B. Effectiveness Review
1. **How is senior leadership effectiveness reviewed?**
- How are leadership goals established?
- What formal procedures are in place to regularly and systematically review leadership practices and effectiveness?
- What mechanisms ensure that effectiveness reviews are used by leaders for professional and organizational improvement?

2. **How is leadership and governance effectiveness reviewed throughout the institution, department, or program?**

- How is informal feedback from colleagues throughout the organization solicited and used?

- What formal, objective, and systematic procedures are in place for reviewing leadership and governance effectiveness at all levels, and how frequently are reviews undertaken?

- How is information gained from the review of leadership and governance disseminated and used for improving leadership systems and practices?

1.2. PUBLIC AND PROFESSIONAL LEADERSHIP

AREAS TO ADDRESS

1. **In what ways do senior leaders—and leaders at all levels—share their expertise and experience with the campus through service on college or university committees, projects, task forces, or other initiatives?**

- What are the types and extent of participation?

- How are decisions made regarding appropriate areas for involvement?

- How is engagement with campus groups and organizations encouraged within the organization, and how is engagement supported and recognized by leaders?

2. **How do senior leaders—and leaders at all levels—share their leadership and disciplinary and/or technical expertise and experience with public, professional, academic, or community groups or organizations?**

- What are the types and extent of participation?

- How are decisions made regarding appropriate areas for involvement?

- How is engagement with public, professional, academic, and/or community groups and organizations encouraged within the organization, and how is it supported and recognized by leaders?

1.3. ETHICS AND SOCIAL RESPONSIBILITY

AREAS TO ADDRESS

A. Ethics and Integrity
1. **Are principles of leadership integrity and ethical behavior clearly defined?**

- How do senior leaders communicate their personal commitment to high standards of ethics and integrity?

- How do senior leaders create awareness of and commitment to those principles and standards among others?

2. **How are areas of potential ethical concern identified?[4] What are those areas, and how are high standards of integrity and ethical behavior ensured in each?**

- How are ethical standards clearly defined, as appropriate, for relations with specific constituencies—including colleagues, students, and members of campus, professional, and academic organizations—and for the general public?

- What methods are used to ensure that appropriate standards of ethical conduct and integrity are widely disseminated and understood?

- What mechanisms are in place for review and compliance monitoring, as appropriate?

- What procedures are in place to ensure that policies and procedures relative to integrity and ethical standards are periodically reviewed, clarified, and updated?

B. Social Responsibility

1. **What are the legal, regulatory, or environmental standards, requirements, and/or risks associated with the organization's work?**

2. **How do leaders ensure that the organization identifies the current and potential legal, regulatory, or environmental impact of its operations on the community and society?[5]**

- What are the areas of potential impact?

- How are they addressed in a proactive manner?

3. **How do leaders ensure that the institution, department, or program maintains consistently high standards in its conformance with pertinent legal, regulatory, and/or environmental standards?**

NOTES

1. *Constituency* refers to any of the beneficiary groups or organizations, stakeholders, consumers, clients, publics, users, or "customers" for which the organization undertakes activities or provides programs or services, or which influence, or are influenced by, the institution, department, or program. Depending on the organization's mission, such services may involve instruction, research or scholarship, public service or outreach, administrative support, or other functions. The list of constituency groups and organizations could include students, faculty, staff, disciplinary and professional communities, potential employers, alumni, academic associations, parents, business and industry, state and federal funding agencies, private foundations and donors, prospective students and parents, graduate and professional schools, advisory boards, disciplinary and administrative opinion leaders at other institutions, local and state government, the citizens of the community, or state and other groups. For administrative departments that serve other departments within the institution—such as departments of human resources, facilities, computing services, or sponsored research; faculty/administrative councils or assemblies; and other administrative and service units—the relevant internal constituencies are the administrative and academic units for which the organization provides

services, and/or which influence or are influenced by the organization. Constituency also refers to any department inside or outside the institution with which the institution, department, or program collaborates. For additional discussion of beneficiaries and constituencies, see Category 3.

2. The terms *organization* and *unit* are used as general terms to refer to an entire institution or an administrative, student life, service, or academic department, program, center, or institute.

3. This may include various documents and channels—print or electronic. The documents may include organizational charts, bylaws, charters, descriptions of policies or procedures, operating manuals, or comparable materials.

4. Examples might include issues related to proprietary rights for information and work products, confidentiality, appropriate treatment of employees, employment practices relative to family members, potential conflicts of interest, academic integrity, financial practices, vendor relations, faculty-student interaction, or other issues of the type raised by the Sarbanes-Oxley Act.

5. Examples might include pollution risks, waste management issues, campus and community safety, parking issues, personal or property security, substance abuse, driver safety, health risks, or laboratory practices.

2.0

PURPOSES AND PLANS

Establishing a clear sense of purpose and developing plans to advance the institution, department, or program in the desired directions are integral to institutional quality and effectiveness. The most fundamental purpose of the planning process is to develop, review, refine, and/or reaffirm the mission, vision, and broad organizational goals; to translate these directions into priorities and action steps; and to see the plans through to completion. A clear statement of purpose and direction is a prerequisite to effective planning. An institution needs "a clear and conscious sense of its essential values and character, its distinctive elements, its place in the higher education community, and its relationship to society at large" (Western Association 2001, 17).

Typically this foundation is provided by a mission statement:

> The mission of the institution defines its distinctive character, addresses the needs of society and identifies the students the institution seeks to serve, and reflects both the institution's traditions and its vision for the future. The institution's mission provides the basis upon which the institution identifies its priorities, plans its future and evaluates its endeavors; it provides a basis for the evaluation of the institution. (New England Association 2004, 3)

The mission statement of an institution, department, or program may identify its future-oriented aspirations, as suggested above, or as is often the case, its vision may be articulated in a separate statement. Whichever approach is taken, the statement, or statements, should indicate what is unique and distinctive about the institution, department, or program and for whom its programs and services are provided. Some organizations also develop a statement of values or operating principles that is viewed as an important foundational document.

As illustrated in Figure 5, the planning process often includes an environmental scan through which current strengths, weaknesses, opportunities, and threats are identified. With these formulations as a backdrop, the planning processes progress to the articulation of measurable goals and the strategies and action plans necessary to their attainment (Tromp and Ruben 2004).[1] The documented plan integrates all these components, ensures that resources are aligned with strategic priorities, and includes a framework for monitoring progress and evaluating outcomes.

FIGURE 5. STEPS IN STRATEGIC PLANNING

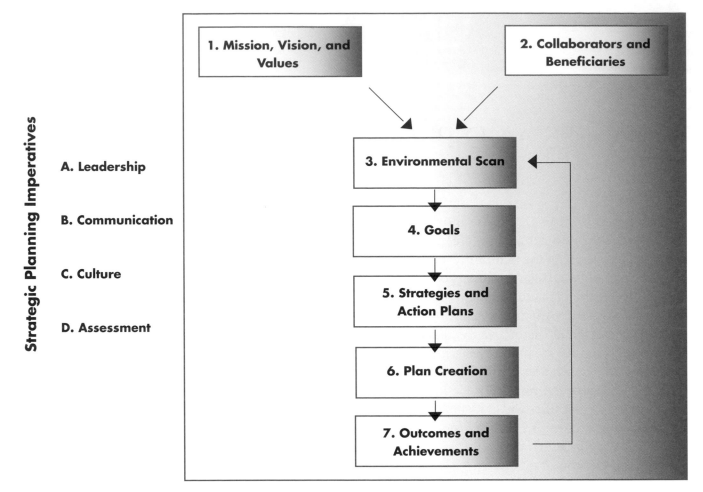

© 2004 Based on Sherrie A. Tromp and Brent D. Ruben, *Strategic Planning in Higher Education: A Leader's Guide*, Washington, D.C.: National Association of College and University Business Officers.

A PLAN AND A PLANNING PROCESS

The goal of strategic planning is the development of a plan that typically includes the steps described above and a process through which the particulars of the plan are developed and implemented. The key steps in "making a plan" and those necessary for "making a plan work" are quite different. Minimally, a successful effort requires that "planning and improvement processes . . . are clearly communicated, provide for constituent participation, and incorporate the use of assessment results" (Middle States Commission 2006, 6). As indicated in Figure 5, leadership, communication, assessment, and cultural considerations are vital to realize this outcome.

2.0. PURPOSES AND PLANS: KEY REVIEW ISSUES

This category focuses on how an institution, department, or program establishes, reviews, refines, and/or reaffirms its sense of purpose and direction, aspirations, short- and long-term goals, and priorities, and its strategies and action plans for achieving them. Also considered is how faculty and staff are engaged in the planning process; how student and/or other constituency groups' needs and expectations are considered; how goals and plans are communicated and coordinated throughout the organization; how progress on goals and plans is assessed; and how follow-through is monitored.

2.1. PLAN DEVELOPMENT

AREAS TO ADDRESS

A. Defined Purpose and Direction

1. Does the institution, department, or program have a clearly defined and shared sense of its purpose (mission), aspirations (vision), and broad organizational goals? Are there published statements or documents that describe the mission and vision? Are there other statements of values, recommended standards of conduct, or operating principles that are important to the institution, department, or program?

2. Do published documents provide accurate, current descriptions of the organization's primary programs and services?
- Do they clearly explain their relationship to the mission and vision?
- Do these statements differentiate this institution, department, or program from others?
- Are these documents current?

B. Documented Plans

1. Does the institution, department, or program have a published strategic plan?
- How, and to whom, is the plan disseminated?
- When was the plan developed?
- Does the plan define broad organizational goals?
- Are those goals clearly linked to the mission and vision?

2. How does the plan translate goals into specific strategies and action plans?

3. Are resource considerations—human, fiscal, facilities, and technical—considered in the plan?

4. Does the plan specify performance indicators and methods for evaluating progress and outcomes?

C. The Planning Process

1. **Is there a formalized planning process?**

- What are the major steps in the process?

- Are the steps and procedures in the process documented?

- How is information about the planning process communicated, and to whom?

- How frequently is the planning cycle undertaken?

2. **How does the planning process take account of:**

- The mission, vision, values, or other foundational documents?

- The needs and expectations of constituency groups served by the institution, department, and/or program?

- Noteworthy challenges and opportunities?

- Relevant trends and issues in higher education, the state, and the region, and pertinent considerations related to economics, technology, regulation, and the marketplace?

- Available resources and the alignment of resources with strategic priorities—fiscal, human, physical facilities, and infrastructure?

- Organizational capabilities, culture, and climate?

3. **How is broad input and participation in the planning process encouraged?**

- How are faculty, staff, students, board members, and/or representatives of other relevant constituency groups engaged in the planning process?

- What communication approaches and channels are used to keep such groups informed and involved during all stages of the planning process?

4. **How is planning coordinated throughout the organization so that the process:**

- Aligns with larger organizational and institutional planning process?

- Establishes clear goals, strategies, and action steps?

- Allocates resources in accordance with strategic priorities?

- Identifies short- and longer-term needs?

- Clarifies responsibilities and responsible individuals or groups for follow-up?

- Ensures flexibility to address unplanned and unanticipated events?

- Identifies appropriate performance indicators and methods for monitoring and assessing outcomes?

- Considers the capabilities and needs of current or potential organizations with which collaboration is important?[4]

- Considers practices and approaches used by peers, competitors, and leaders in the institution and field?[5]

- Provides a useful guide to leaders at all levels for decision making, resource allocation, and the development of new programs or services?

- Provides a mechanism for the prioritization, modification, or termination of programs, services, or other activities that are no longer necessary or effective?

5. **How often is the planning process itself reviewed and improved, and how is that review conducted?**

2.2. PLAN IMPLEMENTATION

AREAS TO ADDRESS

1. **How are faculty, staff, and other constituencies, as appropriate, engaged in the implementation of plans?**
- Are roles and responsibilities clearly defined?
- How are expectations communicated?

2. **How is broad dissemination of and access to information about progress on implementation of plans ensured, and how is shared understanding encouraged?**

3. **How does the organization ensure follow-through on the implementation of its plan to ensure that:**
- Specified goals, strategies, and action steps have been appropriately addressed?
- Appropriate resources are provided?
- Alignment between larger organizational and institutional goals is achieved?
- Short- and longer-term needs have been addressed?
- Implementation responsibilities have been fulfilled?
- Capabilities and needs of current or potential collaborative organizations have been considered?
- Performance indicators and methods for monitoring and assessing outcomes are being used?
- Practices and approaches used by peers, competitors, and leaders have been considered?
- Leaders at all levels are using organizational plans to guide decision making, resource allocation, the development of new programs or services, and the modification or termination of programs and services that are no longer necessary or effective?

4. **How is the implementation of plans synchronized, coordinated, and overseen throughout the organization to ensure that:**
- Key internal and external constituencies are informed and appropriately engaged?
- Resources are allocated in a manner that supports strategic priorities?
- Unanticipated changes in organizational priorities are taken into consideration?

NOTES

1. For a more detailed discussion of the strategic planning model and framework presented here, see Tromp and Ruben (2004).

2. *Mission* refers to the primary work of the unit, the purposes for which the unit exists, including specification of the groups for which the unit provides programs or services.

3. *Vision* refers to a characterization of how the unit sees itself in the future—its broadly expressed, future aspirations, the answer to the question "What would you like your institution, department, or program to be like in 10 years?"

4. *Groups and organizations* with which your organization collaborates include all external groups, departments, programs, institutes, organizations, or agencies that supply human, physical, or financial resources necessary to the work of your organization. For example, high schools, community and junior colleges, and other colleges or universities are providers of students, and potentially of faculty and staff. Vendors of various types supply goods and services. Also included are other units outside your own organization with which alliances, partnerships, joint programs, or shared service arrangements have been formed.

5. Establishing *comparisons*—also termed benchmarking—refers to the process of identifying, selecting, and systematically comparing the organization's performance, programs, services, processes, activities, achievements, and/or impact with those of other programs, departments, and/or institutions. Comparisons may be with higher education organizations and/or with other enterprises that have comparable processes or activities. For example, your approaches to planning may be compared with processes at peer or competitor colleges or universities, or with organizations in other sectors. Comparisons with recognized leaders in higher education and/or with leaders in business, health care, or governmental organizations can provide a basis for innovation for your own organization.

3.0

BENEFICIARIES AND CONSTITUENCIES

Few institutions touch the lives of as many diverse constituencies, directly and indirectly, as colleges and universities. Students are the primary beneficiaries of the work of higher education institutions, and our many academic, student life, and student services have been developed to create a supportive learning and living environment to serve their interests.

A number of other constituencies benefit significantly from the institution's instructional, scholarly, and outreach activities. A list of groups that directly benefit from, influence, or are influenced in one way or another by the work of colleges and universities is a very long one. It includes, in addition to present students, prospective students, alumni, family members, employers, the professional and scholarly community, high schools, other colleges and universities, the local and regional communities, state and federal governments, funding agencies, donors, the mass media, and other groups.

Like the institution as a whole, most departments and programs within it serve students and other external constituency groups. Some programs and departments, however, serve primarily internal groups, and many serve both.

In the first category are academic programs and departments that provide direct benefits to students, alumni, employers, the scholarly and professional communities, the general public, or other external constituencies through teaching, scholarship, and public service.[1] In addition, any number of service and administrative programs and departments—dining, admissions, the registrar, residence life, financial aid, or student affairs, for example—provide important programs and services to students and other external constituencies.

In the second category—programs or services that most directly benefit faculty and staff groups and various internal departments of a college or university—are those provided by departments such as purchasing, budgeting, human resources, payroll, and accounting. Departments that serve both internal and external constituencies include libraries, athletics, the bookstore, computing services, institutional advancement, and university relations.

IDENTIFYING BENEFICIARY AND CONSTITUENCY GROUPS

Units may differ substantially in the kind of work they do, and for whom. However, all college or university programs and departments—and the institution, considered as a whole—have a number of critical beneficiary and constituency groups. Depending on the particular unit and the particular mission, the list of such groups would include one or more of the following:

- Those who benefit from the organization's activities, services, or programs

- Those upon whom the organization's existence depends
- Those who can choose to use or not use the programs or services
- Those who provide resources or expertise essential to the work of the organization
- Those who pay for programs or services
- Those whose assessment of the performance of the programs, services, or activities translates into financial or moral support, or a lack thereof

RELATIONSHIPS WITH BENEFICIARIES AND CONSTITUENCIES

Generally speaking, the most respected organizations across sectors place a great deal of emphasis on developing a clarity as to who their primary beneficiaries and constitutencies are, and in understanding the needs, expectations, and experiences of those individuals, groups, and organizations. They use such insights to prioritize their efforts to form and maintain high-quality, mutually beneficial, and mutually satisfying relationships. Information from beneficiaries and constituencies as to their needs, perspectives, expectations, and experiences is regarded as essential in efforts to evaluate current services and programs, communicate about existing programs and services, identify needed improvements, and create new initiatives.

In leading organizations, systems are put in place to ensure that those within the unit have a clear understanding of the experiences of those whom the programs and services are designed to benefit. The goals are to understand external expectations and priorities, monitor the effectiveness of relationships, identify and address sources of dissatisfaction that may exist, and more generally keep in touch with how the institution, department, or program looks from "outside" the organization (Baldrige 2007a).

Such reasoning and such an approach are also applicable in higher education (AQIP 2005, 2; Baldrige 2007b; Ruben 1995b, 2004). An understanding of the beneficiary and constituency perspective is essential to determine whether the standards of excellence the institution hopes to achieve in its programs and services are being translated into reality in the experiences of those for whom those programs and services were developed. Moreover, in a very practical sense, it is clear that the external judgments of many groups of the quality of a college, university, or department translate into the financial and reputational support that is critical to the work of faculty and staff and the viability of programs, departments, and the institution (Ruben 2004).

Information from beneficiary and constituent groups also helps to identify organizational standards or practices that need improvement but are easily overlooked by "insiders." For instance, when interviewed, students and others often point to the essential role the "frontline" staff of a program or department play in making their experience a negative or positive one. Such people are, in effect, the "face of the organization," the first and often the last—and sometimes the only—point of contact for students, parents, and visitors through personal, telephone, or e-mail contact. Encounters with frontline staff form the basis of impressions that are remembered and repeated many times. Having a clear sense of the perspectives of beneficiaries helps to clarify factors—such as the knowledge and interpersonal sensitivity of frontline staff—that are critical if the good intentions, goals, and aspirations of an institution, department, or program are to be realized.

How does an institution, department, or program ensure that it has an appropriate focus on beneficiaries and constituencies? Generally speaking, the following steps need to be taken:
1. Identify groups for which the organization provides programs, services, materials, or resources. Consider identifying primary and secondary groups, so that prioritization of effort is possible when resources are limited.

2. Use interviews, focus groups, surveys, and other methods to regularly and systematically gather information to gain or validate an understanding of beneficiaries/constituencies' needs, perspectives, expectations, priorities, experiences, and sources of satisfaction and dissatisfaction.[2]

3. Analyze information on unmet needs and expectations, sources of dissatisfaction, and other gap areas.

4. Address significant gaps by improving programs and services, by using communication and education to negotiate new expectations, or by a combination of the two approaches.

In the words of the Academic Quality Improvement Program of the Higher Learning Commission:
> An institution earns the trust, confidence and loyalty of its current and potential students and its other stakeholders... by actively developing and regularly employing listening tools essential for gathering and understanding their diverse and distinctive perspectives. The institution interprets and weighs these expressed needs, preferences, hopes, and requirements to frame ongoing communication, discussion, and refinement of a common mission and vision. Faculty, staff, and administrators integrate this shared focus into their individual work goals and decision-making strategies. (AQIP 2005, 2)

In adopting this approach, it is not assumed that an institution, department, or program should address each and every beneficiary or constituent need, expectation, or concern. Rather, the assumption is simply that this knowledge is one essential input for the planning and priority-setting process. In a practical sense, failing to gather and make use of such information is a great disadvantage to any organization in its effort to fulfill its mission and realize its aspirations, and more fundamentally, it seems at odds with the principles of reflection, analysis, and the advancement of understanding that have long been fundamental values in higher education.

3.0. BENEFICIARIES AND CONSTITUENCIES: KEY REVIEW ISSUES

This category considers how the institution, department, or program learns about the needs, expectations, perspectives, experiences, and satisfaction and dissatisfaction levels of the individuals, groups, and organizations for which programs and services are provided. Also considered is how this information is analyzed and used to create or refine programs or services, and more generally to enhance relationships with beneficiary and constituency groups.[3]

3.1. NEEDS AND EXPECTATIONS

AREAS TO ADDRESS

1. What groups or organizations benefit most directly from the work of the institution, department, or program, and what programs and services are provided for each?

2. What other constituency groups are important to the success of the institution, department, or program—in the sense that they influence, or are influenced by, your organization's work?

3. What is the relative priority of these beneficiary and constituency groups to the fulfillment of the mission, aspirations, goals, and plans? Can they be classified into primary and secondary categories?

4. How does the institution, department, or program learn about the needs, expectations, perspectives, experiences, and sources of satisfaction (or dissatisfaction) of student and/or other beneficiary and constituency groups?

5. What are the most critical needs and expectations of the high-priority beneficiary and constituency groups?

6. How does the organization listen to and learn about the perspectives and decision-making criteria of individuals, groups, or organizations that could have chosen your program or services but did not?[4]

7. What information is gathered, analyzed, and used to anticipate future needs of the groups and organizations for which programs or services are provided? How are the following taken into account:

- Demographic, technological, competitive, societal, environmental, economic, and regulatory factors and trends?

- Insights from current, former, and potential beneficiary or constituency groups for which your organization provides programs or services, or with which your organization collaborates?

- Comparisons with peer, competitor, and leading institutions, departments, or institutions?

3.2. RELATIONSHIP ENHANCEMENT

AREAS TO ADDRESS

1. **How is information about beneficiary and constituent group needs, expectations, experiences, perspectives, and satisfaction levels used to identify and implement improved organizational procedures and practices[5] and stakeholder communication—and ultimately to enhance relationships?**

- How is information on beneficiary and constituent needs and expectations shared?

- How is such information gathered, analyzed, and used to guide improvements in organizational practices and stakeholder communication?

- How is the impact of those improvements monitored and evaluated?

2. **How is basic program or services information communicated to potential and current beneficiaries?[6]**

- How are Web-based and other technologies used to simplify access to and use of information and services?

- How does the organization ensure that people have access to information about particular programs and services at times and places that are convenient and appropriate to their needs?
- How are students, other beneficiaries, the campus community, other important constituent groups, and the general public appropriately informed about improvements?

3. **What are the various face-to-face communication situations[7] through which regular contact occurs between your institution, department, or program and members of your beneficiary or constituency groups?**

- What individuals and groups from your organization have regular and significant contact with members of your beneficiary and constituency groups?

- How does the organization monitor the quality of initial contact and ongoing interactions with those groups to ensure that attentiveness, courtesy, responsiveness, professionalism, and other values and standards are upheld?

4. **What channels are available for people who are seeking special assistance or who want to make suggestions or register complaints? How does the organization ensure prompt and effective follow-up on complaints, suggestions, or other types of feedback?**

NOTES

1. The term *external* is used to refer to constituency groups composed of people not employed by the institution.

2. This assessment might also focus on members of constituencies who *could* be more fully or effectively utilizing your programs and services but are not, so that you may understand the reasons for their decisions. Examples might be undergraduate students who say they know nothing about your advising system, alumni who have regularly given to your program but now have chosen not to contribute, or graduate students you aggressively recruited who selected a program other than yours.

3. *Beneficiary and constituency groups* refers broadly to individuals, groups, or organizations—variously termed stakeholders, users, audiences, consumers, clients, publics, or "customers"—for whom your organization provides programs or services, who benefit directly or indirectly from your work, or who have an important influence on your organization's success. The list of such groups will, of course, depend on the mission of the organization and will be different for academic, student life, administrative, and service organizations. For academic units, the list of such groups and organizations may include students, disciplinary and professional communities, potential employers, alumni, academic associations, business and industry, state and federal funding agencies, private foundations and donors, prospective students and parents, graduate and professional schools, advisory boards, disciplinary and administrative opinion leaders at other institutions, local and state government, the citizens of the community or state, the mass media, and other groups. For administrative departments that provide

programs and services within the institution (such as departments of human resources, facilities, computing services, and sponsored research; faculty/administrative councils or assemblies; and other administrative and service units), the relevant campus groups and organizations are the administrative and academic departments for which the organization provides services (perhaps staff, faculty, or student groups) and in some cases external groups or organizations, such as advisory boards, visitors, families of students, the mass media, and the public.

Note: Faculty and staff are particularly critical constituency groups for all programs, departments, and institutions. They are the sole focus of Category 5 and therefore are not considered in this category.

4. For academic organizations, this might include qualified students who decided not to apply or qualified students who were admitted but elected not to attend an institution or not to enroll in a particular program of study. It might also include faculty or staff who chose not to apply for open positions or rejected positions that were offered, potential sponsors who chose to fund other programs or departments, alumni or contributors who decided not to participate or contribute, or potential collaborators or partnering groups who chose other organizations or options. For business and administrative units, this would include groups and organizations that were eligible or appropriate candidates to use your organization's programs and services but chose other providers.

5. *Organizational procedures and practices* refers to protocols, standards, or guidelines that are established to address the needs and expectations of constituent groups or organizations. Examples include established standards regarding operating hours, waiting times, or response times in replying to e-mails, telephone calls, or letters of complaint.

6. In the case of academic or student life units, for example, how do you inform students about where to find information about policies and requirements, fees, critical deadlines, advisement, student life services and opportunities, learning support resources, available support services, standards of ethics and academic honesty, and where and how inquiries on various topics can be made?

7. Examples might include interaction with faculty or staff during "walk-in" visits in a department office or face-to-face advising sessions.

4.0

PROGRAMS AND SERVICES

Programs and services are the means through which a college or university—and each of its constituent departments, centers, institutes, and other units—gives life to its purposes, aspirations, values, and goals. Through program and service offerings, the expertise of faculty and staff and the other resources of the institution are made available to students, other beneficiary and constituency groups within and outside the university, and society at large.

For the institution as a whole and for many departments within the college or university, a primary focus of any review process is on the effectiveness and efficiency of educational programs and services and how they contribute to college life and learning. The goal, of course, is designing and "enhancing the quality of programs and services within the context of the institution's missions, resources, and capacities, and to create an environment in which teaching, public service, research and learning occur" (Southern Association 2004, 5).

As discussed previously, there are also departments within the college or university that contribute to the institution's purposes and aspirations but whose work is not primarily academic. Examples include human resources, facilities, alumni affairs, accounting, public safety, and computing services. As with the educational departments and programs, however, each of these administrative and service units also has program and service offerings that are an important focus for review and continuing improvement.

Achieving and maintaining high standards in programs and services is an essential and shared goal across academic, student life, administrative, and service departments, and for the institution as a whole. Toward that end, Category 4 focuses on the way in which programs and services of all types are designed, supported, standardized, implemented, evaluated, and continuously improved.

The place to begin is by reviewing the mission, vision, and goals of an institution, department, or program and then asking about how well the current programs and services reflect those purposes, aspirations, and directions. Are they the best expression of the talents and expertise of faculty and/or staff and the potentialities of facilities and resources? Are the programs and services responsive to beneficiary and constituent needs and expectations and to the unique opportunities and challenges that present themselves given the institution's history, location, and other distinctive characteristics and considerations? Are appropriate resources being devoted to them? Are they continuously being improved? Should they be considered as candidates for downsizing or elimination? See Figure 6.

FIGURE 6. RELATIONSHIPS BETWEEN THE INSTITUTION, DEPARTMENTS, AND PROGRAMS AND SERVICES

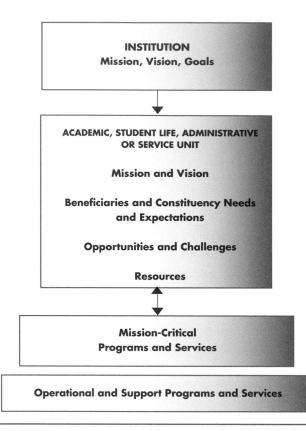

MISSION-CRITICAL PROGRAMS AND SERVICES

Mission-critical programs and services are those that are essential to the work of the institution, department, or program and to the purposes for which the organization was created. For educational units, the mission-critical programs and services at most institutions are those related directly to teaching/learning, scholarship, and public service/outreach.

Regular review of educational programs and services is essential from a variety of perspectives. While common aspirations for college and university students exist, it is important that institutions and programs periodically undergo a process of reviewing their desired learning [and other] outcomes, taking ownership of them, and assuring that they guide practice. (Association of American Colleges and Universities 2004, 5)

In student life, administrative, and service organizations, the programs, services, and desired outcomes will vary substantially from department to department, reflecting the unit's specific mission. Regardless of the type of organization, meaningful review and ongoing improvement presuppose that the programs and services offered have defined goals. Clear goals help promote effective communication with beneficiaries and constituencies, foster better alignment of expectations among all parties, and provide the necessary foundation for assessment. As is discussed in greater detail under Category 6, organizational goals provide the reference point against which the quality and effectiveness of current activities, accomplishments, and outcomes of a program, department, and/or institution can be assessed.

OPERATIONAL AND SUPPORT SERVICES

For the institution as a whole, as well as for the numerous academic, student life, administrative, and service departments that compose it, a number of behind-the-scenes operational and support activities provide the infrastructure necessary to support the mission-critical work. Often these kinds of programs and services are invisible to external groups. For example, support services might include recruiting and hiring, conducting personnel reviews, training, procurement of equipment and supplies, coordinating repairs and maintenance, budgeting, grant writing and management, time and room scheduling, preparing work materials, and planning meetings.

PROCESSES

Whether one thinks of mission-critical or operational and support activities, it is often the case, as the popular adage points out, that "the devil is in the details." That is to say, the overall quality of any program or service is largely a by-product of the effectiveness and efficiency of a number of specific sequences of activities—or *processes*—and how those come together. Figure 7 illustrates these relationships.

FIGURE 7. PROGRAMS, SERVICES, AND PROCESSES

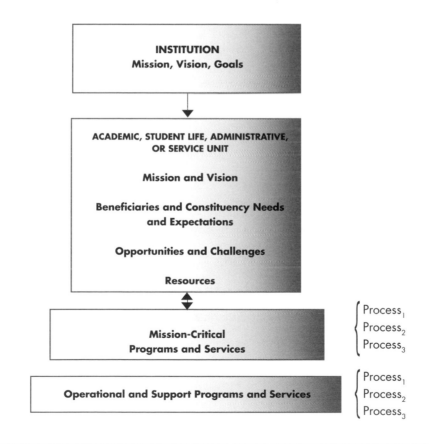

To be most useful, a review should both broadly focus on programs and services and closely examine the key processes that go into making a program or service what it is. In the case of academic programs and services, for example, one can identify and examine a number of processes that are important to teaching/learning, scholarship, and service/outreach, a sampling of which are listed in Figure 8.

The careful review of processes to be sure that they "add value" is increasingly becoming an important criterion for accreditation review, as it long has been for Baldrige-based assessment (Association of American Colleges and Universities 2004; Baldrige 2006; Middle States Commission 2006; Southern Association 2006; North Central Association 2007). A review should, therefore, not only focus on the effectiveness of a program or service overall but also consider the extent to which associated processes are thoughtfully designed, appropriately supported, sufficiently standardized and documented, efficiently implemented, periodically evaluated, and regularly improved, as well as whether they meet constituent needs and expectations.

FIGURE 8. EDUCATIONAL PROGRAMS AND SERVICES AND EXAMPLES OF ASSOCIATED PROCESSES

Program/Service: Teaching/Learning

Associated Processes
- Defining program and course goals
- Developing new courses
- Delivering courses
- Appointing, supervising, and reviewing teaching effectiveness (part-time, adjunct, other instructors)
- Advising students
- Reviewing teaching and providing input to review faculty members for promotion and tenure
- Establishing and reviewing discipline/department procedures and requirements protocols
- Assessing learning outcomes

Program/Service: Scholarship

Associated Processes
- Seeking support for research
- Supporting research and scholarly activity (financial resources, travel, facilities)
- Developing opportunities for faculty/student research collaboration
- Managing research facilities and personnel
- Facilitating interdepartmental and/or interinstitutional collaboration
- Disseminating scholarly publications

Program/Service: Outreach and Public Service

Associated Processes
- Developing community outreach initiatives (alumni, prospective students, legislators, corporate partners)
- Advancing the use of faculty expertise
- Promoting volunteerism
- Developing collaborative relationships with other institutions
- Partnering with other sectors

FIGURE 9. OPERATIONAL AND SUPPORT SERVICES AND EXAMPLES OF ASSOCIATED PROCESSES

Operational/Support Activities

Associated Processes

- Budgeting and managing financial processes
- Developing and overseeing contractual arrangements (government, industry, other organizations)
- Coordinating resources (financial, building, fiscal)
- Allocating and evaluating space and resources
- Ordering equipment
- Developing and overseeing procedures for maintaining records (reliability, confidentiality, accessibility, security)
- Managing computer technology and applications

This review framework and all of the same considerations apply to a review of operational and support programs, services, and associated processes, examples of which are shown in Figure 9. For these activities, to at least as great an extent as for mission-critical programs and services, details of specific processes are critical to overall effectiveness and efficiency.

PROCESS ANALYSIS

A review of programs and services involves identifying and analyzing mission-critical work and associated processes. It also includes an analysis of important operational and support services, and the processes associated with those areas. But how does one analyze a process? For illustrative purposes, consider an academic department that has teaching/learning as a central element of its mission. Various programs and services are developed within the department to fulfill the instructional mission, and those have a number of associated processes that can be examined. One such process is that involved in developing new courses.

To analyze the effectiveness and efficiency of a process, it is helpful to develop a flow chart that identifies and describes the various steps involved. Figure 10 provides an example of a flow chart of the steps required for the approval of a new course in a hypothetical department. Dissecting a process in this way helps to clarify its details, determine how well it works, and potentially improve its functioning, as well. In this case, the process analysis reveals reasons why it takes so long to introduce a new course at the institution. As it presently operates, one can imagine that the process satisfies institutional needs for careful review. However, if achieving this result takes a year because of the process's complexity, the needs and expectations of faculty, students, and perhaps employers may not be well served. Systematic study can help determine whether steps could be shortened or eliminated, procedures streamlined, technology introduced to expedite reviews and approvals, and so on. An analysis of this kind generally results in improved processes—processes that are more efficient, more effective, and more responsive to the needs of all parties involved. Ideally, this approach also results in key processes that are sufficiently documented and standardized so that they can be easily described, understood, utilized, and consistently replicated.

FIGURE 10. SAMPLE FLOW CHART: THE PROCESS FOR DEVELOPING A NEW COURSE

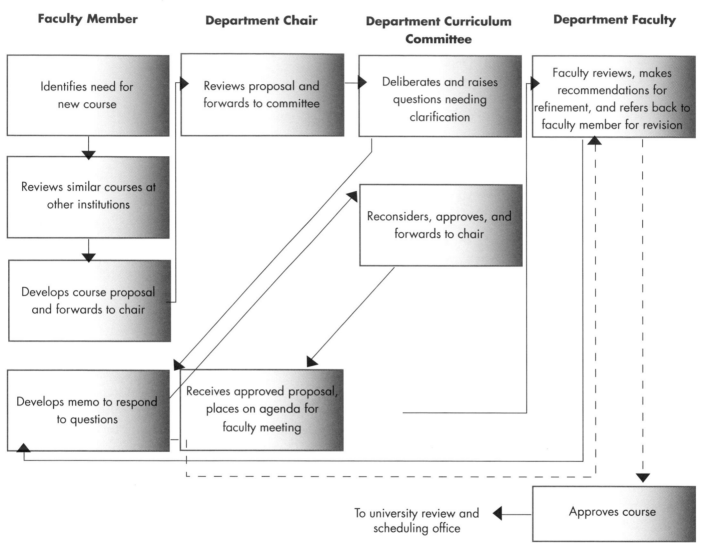

PROGRAM AND INSTRUCTION
ASSOCIATED PROCESS DEVELOPING A NEW COURSE

INTERDEPARTMENTAL AND CROSS-FUNCTIONAL PROCESSES

In some cases, processes require collaboration with external groups and organizations. Figure 11 provides a process view of how various academic, student life, administrative, and service departments come into play during the institutional life-cycle of a student. In the illustration in Figure 11, cross-functional and collaborative relationships between academic, student life, administrative, and service departments are important to effectively and efficiently integrate the student experience. In some instances, integrated interdepartmental processes are created through careful coordination of services; in other instances, that goal may be achieved through cross-training and/or collocating staff; and in still other circumstances, technology can be utilized to facilitate seamless coordination of programs and services.

FIGURE 11. A FUNCTIONAL—INTERDEPARTMENTAL—VIEW OF THE STUDENT EXPERIENCE

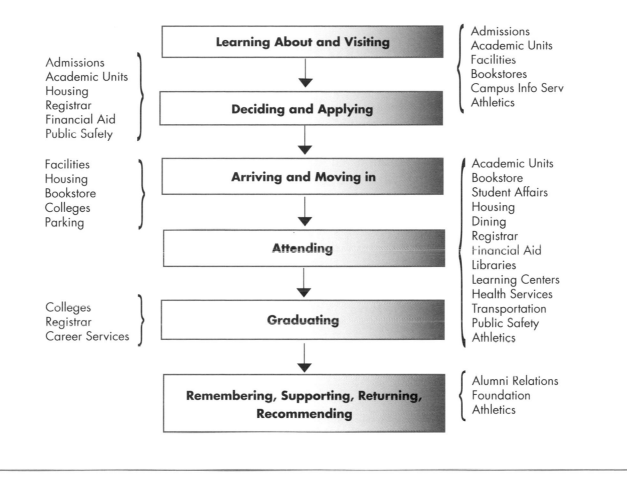

Alliances, service agreements, partnerships, and other forms of collaborative relationships also take place at the institutional level. Examples include recruiting and transfer processes involving high schools and community and junior colleges; cooperative instruction or research arrangements with other institutions or departments; shared service agreements; and arrangements creating preferred or exclusive provider-supplier relationships for programs, materials, resources, or services. As in other instances, careful examination of cross-functional and interdepartmental programs and services—and their associated processes—is a useful aspect of program, department, or institutional review efforts.

COMPARISONS

Comparisons between one's own programs and services and those in other departments or institutions are an essential component of review and improvement—in academic as well as student life, service, and administrative areas. Most broadly, comparisons provide a context for reviewing the nature, content, and effectiveness of programs, services, and their associated processes. At the same time, comparisons generate new ideas, approaches, and methods that can be adopted or adapted.

Leading organizations in other sectors are quite aggressive in their efforts to analyze and learn from peers, competitors, and leaders in their own field and sector, and also in others. This posture can be just as helpful in higher education.

4.0. PROGRAMS AND SERVICES: KEY REVIEW ISSUES

Category 4 focuses on the programs, services, and associated processes that are essential to accomplishing and advancing the institution's, department's, and/or program's mission. Also considered are important support and operational activities and processes. In each case, the focus is on how the programs and services—and associated processes—are designed, supported, standardized, implemented, evaluated, and improved to ensure that high standards are achieved.

4.1. MISSION-CRITICAL PROGRAMS, SERVICES, AND PROCESSES

AREAS TO ADDRESS

1. **What are the mission-critical programs and services—and the most important associated processes—of the institution, department, or program?**

- How is each program or service related to the mission, vision, and broad organizational goals?
- What beneficiary and constituency groups[1] are served by specific programs and services?
- What are the specific goals and intended outcomes of each program or service?[2]
- For each program or service area, what are the most critical associated processes?[3]

2. **How does your organization ensure that each mission-critical program, service, and associated process is of high quality? What approaches are used to determine whether appropriate standards are met in:**

- *Designing* new program or service offerings?
- *Supporting* programs and services with appropriate fiscal, technical, human, and physical resources?
- *Standardizing and documenting* processes and procedures to ensure an appropriate level of reliability and consistency?
- *Delivering* programs and services, and their associated processes?
- *Evaluating* program, service, and process outcomes?
- *Improving* current offerings, *discovering* possibilities for new or refined programs and services, and *identifying* programs or services no longer needed in their present form that can be restructured or eliminated?

3. How does your organization review the quality and effectiveness of program and service offerings, and of their associated processes, and how is the information that results used for improvement?

- How do you determine whether programs and services are achieving their goals and intended outcomes?
- How are the results of assessment used to provide feedback, as appropriate, to beneficiaries and constituencies?
- How are assessments used to guide review and improvement, or if appropriate, for the restructuring or eliminating of program and service offerings, or of particular processes?

4. How does the organization ensure that new and existing programs and services, and their associated processes, benefit from the latest and most appropriate technological innovations?

5. What groups or organizations play a critical role as partners or collaborators with mission-critical processes, and how are high standards of quality established and maintained in collaborative work with those organizations?

6. How are peer, competitor, and leading organizations in the institution or field selected for purposes of comparative review, what organizations are used for that purpose, and how is the information derived from such comparisons used in monitoring, assessment, improvement, or restructuring?

7. How often are mission-critical programs and services formally reviewed? How is that done, and by whom?

4.2. OPERATIONAL AND SUPPORT SERVICES—AND THEIR PROCESSES

AREAS TO ADDRESS

1. What are your key operational and support services, and their associated processes?

- How is each necessary to support mission-critical programs and services?
- For each operational and support service, what are the most critical associated processes?[4]

2. How do you determine whether your operational and support services, and associated processes, are effective and efficient, and how is that information used for improving these services—or, if appropriate, restructuring, combining, or eliminating services?

3. **What approaches are used to achieve and maintain quality in each operational and support service—and in the associated processes? How does your organization ensure that high standards are met in:**

- *Designing* new services?

- *Supporting* services with appropriate fiscal, technical, human, and physical resources?

- *Standardizing and documenting* processes and procedures to ensure an appropriate level of reliability and consistency?

- *Delivering* operational or support services and their associated processes?

- *Evaluating* service and process outcomes?

- *Improving* current offerings, *discovering* possibilities for new or refined programs and services, and *identifying* programs or services that can be restructured or eliminated?

4. **How does the organization ensure that new and existing operational and support services and their associated processes benefit from the latest and most appropriate technological innovations?**

5. **What groups or organizations play a critical role as partners or collaborators for operational and support services and processes, and how do you ensure that high standards of quality are established and maintained in collaborative work with those organizations?**

6. **How are peer, competitor, and leading organizations in the institution or field selected for purposes of comparative review, what organizations are used for that purpose, and how is the information gained from comparisons used in monitoring, assessment, improvement, or restructuring?**

7. **How often are your operational and support areas and processes formally reviewed? How is that done and by whom?**

NOTES

1. *Beneficiary and constituency groups* refers broadly to individuals, groups, or organizations—variously termed stakeholders, users, audiences, consumers, clients, publics, or "customers"—for whom you provide programs or services, who benefit directly or indirectly from your work, or who have an important influence on your organization's success. The list of such groups will, of course, depend on the mission of the institution, department, or program and will be different for academic, student life, administrative, or service organizations. For academic units, the list of such groups and organizations may include students, disciplinary and professional communities, potential employers, alumni, academic associations, parents, business and industry, state and federal funding agencies, private foundations and donors, prospective students and parents, graduate and professional schools, advisory boards, disciplinary and administrative opinion lead-

ers at other institutions, local and state government, the citizens of the community or state, the mass media, and other groups. For administrative departments that provide programs and services within the institution (such as departments of human resources, facilities, computing services, and sponsored research; faculty/administrative councils or assemblies; and other administrative and service units), the relevant campus groups and organizations are the administrative and academic departments for which the organization provides services (perhaps staff, faculty, or student groups) and in some cases external groups or organizations, such as advisory boards, visitors, families of students, the mass media, and the public.

Note: Faculty and staff are critical constituency groups for all programs, departments, and institutions, and as such they are the theme of Category 5, which focuses on individuals employed within an institution, department, or program. Therefore, faculty and staff are not considered in this category.

2. For academic and student life departments, goals would address outcomes related to teaching/learning, scholarship/research, and public service/outreach. In administrative areas, the focus would be on outcomes directly related to the mission-critical work of the unit.

3. *Process* refers to the sequences of work activities that are associated with fulfillment of an institution, department, or program mission and related activities, programs, and services. Processes associated with mission-critical programs and services are those for which the organization has particular expertise. For academic units, mission-critical work processes typically include activities directly associated with teaching/learning, scholarship/research, and service/outreach. In administrative organizations, mission-critical processes will vary greatly depending on the unit's mission but in each case will also relate to the core expertise of the department.

4. Operational and support services and processes are necessary to assist in the fulfillment of the mission and in the development and implementation of programs and services. Often such processes are invisible to external groups—for example, fiscal management, budgeting, managing grants, recruiting and hiring, conducting performance reviews, training, purchasing equipment and supplies, coordinating repairs and maintenance, time and room scheduling, preparing work materials, scheduling and conducting meetings, and so on.

5.0

FACULTY/STAFF AND WORKPLACE

The work of recruiting, developing, and retaining outstanding faculty and staff is critical in any college or university. Perhaps more so than in many other organizations, the people who work in higher education determine the quality of the programs and services that can be offered. Faculty expertise forms the basis for teaching/learning, scholarship/research, and service/outreach. And together, faculty and staff create and maintain a learning and living environment in which knowledge is created, shared, and applied in various forms and contexts for many groups.

The kind of institution that faculty and staff together create is, in itself, a powerful teaching tool. The role of the faculty is obvious. However, important lessons are taught not only in the classroom by faculty but also by the way the institution, departments, and programs are organized and operate, and by staff, through each encounter with students and colleagues (Light 2001; Ruben 2004). Even in non-academic departments, the staff members at all levels throughout a department or institution are often an important source to the teaching, image, and reputation of an institution, department, or program. Together with the faculty, staff play an essential role in maintaining high-quality programs and services (Ruben 1995c).

Because the mission of colleges and higher education is so dependent on faculty and staff, no objective is more crucial than that of creating the kind of workplace culture, climate, and practices that encourage, recognize, and reward excellence, innovation, and professional development. In any college or university environment, the challenge is to encourage faculty and staff to develop their disciplinary and technical capabilities while also contributing meaningfully to the institution's mission, vision, goals, and plans. For faculty who are members of disciplinary and professional communities—as well as the campus community—it is particularly important to create a climate that is engaging, and personally and professionally satisfying, in order to fully engage them in the life of the institution.

This category considers factors that contribute to creating a superior workplace and outstanding, well-trained, engaged, collaborative, and committed faculty and staff members. Issues related to faculty and staff focus on standards and orientation, review and recognition, learning and professional development, and satisfaction assessment. Consideration of workplace practices includes organizational structure, position and responsibilities, and workplace environment and climate.

5.0. FACULTY/STAFF AND WORKPLACE: KEY REVIEW ISSUES

5.1. FACULTY AND STAFF

A. **Standards and Orientation**
   1. **What approaches are used to recruit, select, and retain faculty and/or staff?** [1]

   - How does the institution, department, or program identify its faculty and/or staff needs?

   - How are the necessary faculty and/or staff credentials and competencies determined?

   - What methods are used for recruiting and selecting faculty and/or staff?

   - How are standards and expectations for candidates for open positions established and communicated?

   - What methods are used to ensure the retention of outstanding faculty and/or staff?

   2. **What kinds of orientation programs and/or mentoring experiences are provided for new faculty and/or staff? For what groups are these provided, and by whom?**

   3. **How is basic job-related information provided relative to:**
   - Salary and benefits?
   - Core competencies for jobs?
   - Performance reviews and promotion processes?
   - Standards of ethics and integrity?
   - Diversity and discrimination?
   - Institutional regulations, practices, and policies?
   - Grievances and internal disputes?
   - Required training and certifications?

B. **Review and Recognition** [2]
   1. **How do performance review procedures operate to ensure useful and timely feedback for faculty and staff groups?**

   2. **How are review and recognition systems and practices used to encourage, recognize, and reward superior performance?**

   3. **How do compensation, benefits, and related reward and incentive practices support and reinforce organizational directions and priorities?**

4. How are nonfinancial rewards, practices, and/or events used to recognize individual and collective excellence, and to reinforce organizational directions and priorities?

5. How, and how often, does the organization formally review its performance review and recognition systems?

C. Learning and Professional Development
1. How does the institution, department and/or program identify the competencies and capabilities needed by faculty and/or staff? How is each of the following taken into account:
- Directions, aspirations, priorities, goals, and plans of the organization?
- The needs, capabilities, and perspectives of faculty/staff?
- Job performance review outcomes?
- Requirements for certification, licensure, or accreditation?
- Changing technology?
- Evolving institutional or marketplace needs and expectations?

2. What personal and professional learning and development[3] opportunities are provided for faculty and/or staff groups?
- How is participation in program, department, campus, and other development activities and events encouraged for each faculty and staff group?
- What leadership and skill development opportunities are provided?
- How is career development guidance provided?

3. What approaches are used to deliver professional education and development?[4]

4. How are professional education and development opportunities evaluated, and how are results used for improvement?

5. How are special education and training needs, such as leadership development, technology training, diversity awareness, crisis management, trades training, ESL, and GED, addressed as appropriate? Who is responsible for providing the resources for such training, and how are these programs evaluated?

D. Faculty and Staff Well-Being and Satisfaction
1. How does the institution, department, and/or program learn about the faculty and staff experience and faculty and staff needs, expectations, and sources of satisfaction and dissatisfaction?[5]

2. **How is information related to faculty and staff and workplace satisfaction/dissatisfaction used to enhance organizational practices and the quality of the working environment more generally?**
   - How is this information gathered, analyzed, and shared?
   - How is information used to guide planning and improvement?
   - How are the improvement process and its outcomes monitored and evaluated?

3. **How, and how often, does your organization formally review its approaches to faculty and staff satisfaction assessment?**

5.2. WORKPLACE

AREAS TO ADDRESS

A. **Structure**
   1. **What is the organizational and leadership structure of the institution, department, and/or program?**
      - What are the reporting relationships among the units?
      - What is the size of each of the major areas or work groups within the organization?
      - What is the primary function of each?

   2. **How does the organization determine the appropriateness of particular organizational and leadership structures for:**
      - Advancing the mission and aspirations?
      - Effectively utilizing faculty/staff capabilities?
      - Ensuring appropriate engagement opportunities for faculty and/or staff?
      - Managing resources and workload equitably?
      - Considering the needs and expectations of beneficiaries, constituencies, faculty, and staff?
      - Aligning with national standards for functional operations (e.g., Council for the Advancement of Standards in Higher Education)?[6]
      - Ensuring proper controls to maintain operational integrity (e.g., financial, personnel, and information technology)?

   3. **How does your institution, department, or program review and improve its organizational structure?**
      - How and when was the current structure established?
      - Is there a procedure for periodically reviewing organizational structures? What are the steps in that process, and how often does a review take place?
      - What changes or refinements have been made within the past five years?
      - What other structures have been considered or implemented?

B. Positions and Responsibilities
   1. How does the institution, department, or program develop and communicate position descriptions, associated responsibilities, and performance standards?

   2. How does your organization design, organize, and oversee work practices to encourage:
   - Individual excellence?
   - Departmental and institutional excellence?
   - Collegiality and teamwork?
   - Collaboration?
   - Innovation?
   - Valuing diversity (including age, race, ethnicity, and gender)?
   - Appreciation of institutional and departmental ethical standards?

   3. How is organizational flexibility encouraged? For instance, how are the following used:
   - Cross-training?
   - Redesign of work processes?
   - Job rotation?
   - Technology?
   - Simplification and reduction of job classifications?

C. Workplace Environment and Climate
   1. What approaches does the program, department, and/or institution use to maintain a healthy, safe, and secure work environment?

   2. How does the organization identify improvement needs and monitor progress in the areas of health, safety, and security?

   3. What approaches are used to ensure that the institution, department, or program maintains appropriate health and safety standards and/or regulatory requirements relative to:
   - Human resources?
   - Physical resources?
   - Equipment?
   - Electronic services and products?
   - Laboratories?
   - Computers?

4. **How does the organization ensure workplace preparedness for emergencies or disasters?**[7]
   - Are plans in place for reacting in the case of an emergency or disaster?
   - How are those plans shared, tested, and periodically reviewed and updated?

5. **What approaches are used to create a positive and congenial workplace climate?**

6. **How does the program, department, and/or institution promote and reward collegiality, collaboration, and teamwork among faculty and staff groups?**

7. **How does the organization learn about faculty/staff perceptions of workplace climate, and how is that information used for improvement?**

8. **How, and how often, are approaches to workplace climate assessment formally reviewed and refined?**

NOTES

1. The phrase faculty and/or staff is used to refer to all salaried employee groups. This includes full- and part-time faculty, teaching assistants, coadjutant faculty, visiting lecturers, full- and part-time administration and staff, and student workers.

2. Recognition includes, but is not limited to, public acknowledgment of individuals and groups/teams, personal feedback, and merit awards. Also included are letters of commendation, certifications of merit, articles in bulletins or newsletters, or announcements at meetings.

3. This might include sabbaticals, internships, professional development programs, or flex-time before or after work to permit enrollment in professional development activities.

4. This might include orientations, traditional academic courses, computer-based instruction, distance education, on-campus programs, off-campus programs, consultants, or self-paced instruction.

5. Faculty/staff satisfaction and workplace climate might be assessed through surveys or interviews, retention rates, absenteeism, grievance rates, analysis of exit interviews, or other indicators established by the organization. Further discussion of assessment, comparisons, and outcomes is provided in categories 6 and 7.

6. See the Council for the Advancement of Standards in Higher Education at http://www.cas.edu/.

7. For example, natural disasters, crimes on campus, campus unrest, terrorist activity, or loss of core institutional functions such as information technology support.

6.0

ASSESSMENT AND INFORMATION USE

As the preceding sections of this guide have made clear, leadership, purposes and plans, beneficiaries and constituencies, programs and services, and faculty/staff and workplace climate are all essential elements of institutional, departmental, and/or programmatic quality and effectiveness. Category 6 focuses on how progress, achievements, and outcomes are assessed in each of those areas. Category 7 considers what the results of assessment show.

In addition, this category looks at how you determine which peer, competitive, or leading organizations to use for comparative assessment of your outcomes and achievements. Finally, the category addresses how you make use of the information gained through assessment, and more generally how the expertise and experience of faculty and staff, is shared and used to improve the quality and effectiveness of your institution, department, and/or program.

INCREASING ATTENTION TO ASSESSMENT

Assessing and using outcome information has always been a fundamental theme of the Baldrige framework, and in recent years it has become an increasingly central topic within accreditation. Indeed, one of the primary goals of accreditation is described as "promoting within institutions a culture of evidence where indicators of performance are regularly developed and data collected to inform institutional decision making, planning, and improvement" (Western Association 2001, 8).

Reflecting this perspective, the primary emphasis of Category 6 is on how the institution, department, or program approaches assessment, or in other words, how "the institution engages in ongoing, integrated, and institution-wide research-based planning and evaluation processes that incorporate a systematic review of programs and services that (a) results in continuing improvement, and (b) demonstrates that the institution is effectively accomplishing its mission" (Southern Association 2006).

Beyond assessment's importance for the purposes of evaluation and planning, a unit often reaps a number of far-reaching benefits from a thoughtfully planned and executed program of assessment (Kaplan and Norton 1996, 2001; Ruben 2004). They include the following:

- Stimulating dialogue and clarifying the organization's mission, aspirations, and priorities

- Heightening the shared sense of the purposes of programs and services

- Developing a shared perspective on the appropriate standards and indicators of excellence

- Identifying current strengths

- Clarifying improvement needs

- Providing meaningful comparisons

- Heightening personal and collective responsibility

- Encouraging, monitoring, and documenting progress

- Providing a foundation for fact-based planning, decision making, and problem solving

- Energizing and motivating faculty and staff

- Providing the basis for more effective communication about institutional, departmental, or programmatic strengths

To achieve such benefits, the assessment planning and implementation process must be undertaken in a way that appropriately engages members of the organization in determining what to measure and why, and how to use the results. Such a process heightens the ownership and perceived value of the assessment process and its results.

STEPS IN THE ASSESSMENT PROCESS

Typically, the assessment process begins with the decision about the appropriate focus for review. Will it be leadership, purposes and plans, beneficiaries and constituencies, programs and services, faculty/staff and workplace, or assessment and information sharing? In each case, the basic question is: "How do we know whether we are succeeding in achieving our aims in this area?" The challenge, then, is to decide what information and evidence the organization needs to make its determinations, how to gather that information, what useful data may already be available, and ultimately how to gather, integrate, and use the various sources of information and evidence to document outcomes, determine progress, and guide improvement.

The specifics and language of course vary somewhat depending on the nature of the unit involved. But broadly stated, here are the steps:

1. Define or clarify goals.

2. Assess outcomes and achievements relative to these goals, including comparisons of outcomes over time, with peers, and with other institutions and organizations.

3. Monitor and use results for determining outcomes and achievements, informing day-to-day decision making and resource allocation, and improving the quality and effectiveness of the institution, department, and/or program.

Regardless of whether the assessment process is undertaken for an entire institution or a specific academic, student life, administrative, or service department or program, the objective is to integrate the process into the life of the organization.

Figure 12 provides a more detailed description of the steps involved in establishing an integrated assessment framework.[1]

FIGURE 12. STEPS TO DEVELOP AN INTEGRATED ASSESSMENT PROCESS

1. **Define or Clarify Goals**
   - Identify and consider the needs and expectations of beneficiaries and constituencies and other key factors.
   - Establish clear and shared goals for program and service areas and offerings.
   - Be certain that goals cover the full range of relevant activities.
   - Clearly communicate goals to beneficiaries and constituencies.

2. **Evaluate Outcomes**
   - Use established goals to guide assessment activities at all levels in your instiution, department, and/or program.
   - Develop and use appropriate outcome indicators, criteria, measures, and evaluative procedures.
   - Assess the extent to which established goals are being met within program and service areas and more generally, and identify gaps.
   - Assess progress by examining patterns and trends.
   - Make comparisons with peers at other institutions.
   - Confirm that assessment covers all defined goals, and other factors associated with institutional effectiveness.

3. **Use the Assessment Outcome Information**
   - Communicate the results of assessment to colleagues within the institution, and to beneficiary and constituency groups, as appropriate.
   - Compare outcome information, as appropriate, with results from previous years and with those from peer, competitor, and/or leading institutions to identify improvement targets.
   - Use outcome information to improve programs and services, and the effectiveness of the institution, department, and/or program more generally.
   - Integrate outcome information into formal and informal planning and decision-making activities.
   - Periodically review and, as appropriate, refine and update your goals, assessment procedures, and approaches to using this information.

INSTITUTIONAL ASSESSMENT

Institution-level assessment provides the broadest view of the effectiveness of a college or university. Figure 13 illustrates how the EHE framework applies to assessment at this level. The scheme includes the same themes that are embodied in the standards and principles for institutional assessment in accrediting models. The Middle States approach, for example, includes a focus on mission and goals, leadership and governance, planning and resources, and assessment, among others (Middle States Commission 2006). Issues related to programs and services and faculty are also addressed, within the category of educational effectiveness (Middle States Commission 2006).

FIGURE 13. INSTITUTIONAL EFFECTIVENESS ASSESSMENT

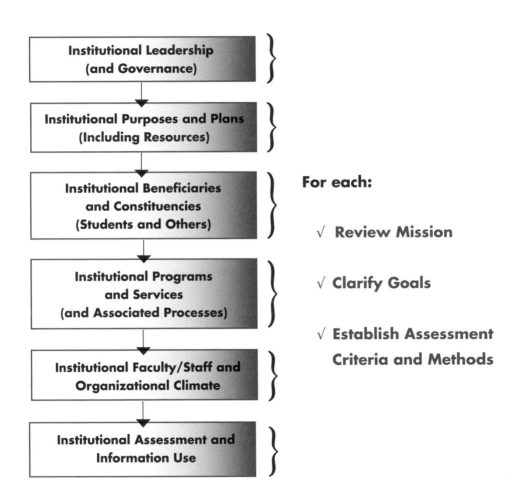

ASSESSMENT IN ADMINISTRATIVE AND SERVICE DEPARTMENTS

One can also use this same framework as a guide for assessment in any academic, student life, administrative, or service unit within a college or university. This unit-level approach to assessment is extremely useful for helping to determine and document how effective specific programs or departments are in fulfilling their mission and achieving critical goals.

Within administrative or service departments, assessment focuses on how the work of the departments fulfills their administrative or service mission and goals and also, where applicable, how their activities contribute to student learning outcomes. For such departments, an array of indicators and measures is available. The choice of which to select depends on the department's purposes, aspirations, and broad organizational goals, as well as the nature of its programs and services. Figure 14 shows a sampling of potential indicators.

FIGURE 14. POTENTIAL ASSESSMENT INDICATORS FOR ADMINISTRATIVE AND SERVICE DEPARTMENTS

Leadership

- Effectiveness ratings by colleagues and peers
- Performance review results
- Progress on leadership priorities and projects
- Contributions to campus, community, and professional organizations

Purposes and Plans

- Progress on review of mission and vision
- Progress in establishing a formalized strategic planning process
- Progress on plans and goals

Mission-Critical Programs and Services

- Effectiveness
- Efficiency
- Reliability
- Cycle time
- Resource utilization

Beneficiary and Constituency Relations

- Service user satisfaction ratings
- Focus group results
- Satisfaction with programs and services
- Positive and improving reputation for quality and service

Operational and Support Services

- Financial management effectiveness
- Staff recruiting and training effectiveness
- Policy and regulation adherence
- Adequacy of technology
- Effectiveness and efficiency of equipment and facilities management

Faculty/Staff and Workplace Satisfaction

- Recruitment
- Attractiveness
- Turnover/retention
- Compensation
- Organizational culture and climate
- Morale
- Professional courses/programs offered/taken
- Recognition provided

Assessment and Information Sharing

- Rating of progress in developing assessment system
- Implementation of new assessment tools or methods
- Dissemination of assessment results
- Use of outcomes information of improvement

FIGURE 15. ASSESSMENT OF EDUCATIONAL PROGRAMS, SERVICES, AND PROCESSES

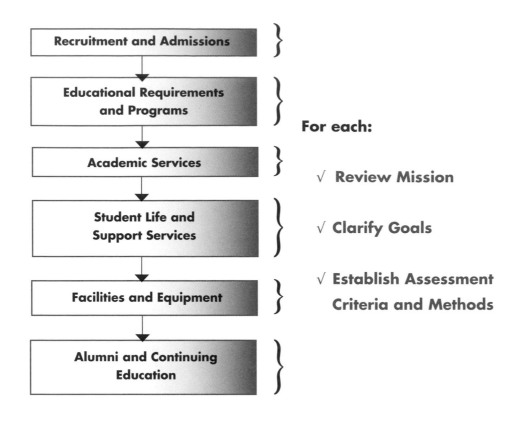

ASSESSMENT IN EDUCATIONAL DEPARTMENTS AND PROGRAMS

As with the assessment of an institution as a whole or of administrative or service units, assessment within educational departments focuses on departmental leadership, purposes and plans, beneficiaries and constituencies, programs and services, faculty/staff and workplace, and assessment and information sharing.

For departments that have a curricular or co-curricular teaching/learning mission, assessing learning outcomes is a priority. The basic questions in assessing learning outcomes are these:

- What are we trying to accomplish through our program's courses and the learning opportunities and living experiences we provide?

- What do we want students who graduate from our institution/department/program to know and be able to do?

- How do we assess our effectiveness in achieving these outcomes, and what do the results tell us?

- How can we use information gained through assessment to improve our programs, services, and their associated processes?

This assessment process might focus on a general education curriculum and/or student life programs and services, on offerings within a single academic department (e.g., major or minor programs, individual courses), or on all of these.

Alternatively, assessment might be interdepartmental and cross-functional and organized to reflect the phases of a student's experience. As illustrated in Figure 15, a number of educational, student life, and student services functions play a role in the student living and learning experience, and assessment can be undertaken in a way that seeks to document how the work of each of these units contributes to the creation of learning opportunities for students and to student learning as they progress through an institution.

Regardless of the approach one selects, assessing educational programs and services includes a consideration of the learning opportunities provided by the various educational, student life, and service units or functions illustrated in Figure 15. Each function is composed of a number of processes that are important to the satisfactory progress of students through the institution, and each can be assessed in terms of its contributions to the quality of the student experience and learning outcomes and other established goals, as described in Figure 16.

FIGURE 16. ASSESSING TEACHING AND LEARNING OUTCOMES IN EDUCATIONAL PROGRAMS

1. Define Student Learning Goals

- Consider student needs and expectations, as well as other key issues.

- Establish clear and shared goals for specific educational programs, services, courses, and stages (e.g., the "first-year experience," "major," or "capstone experience").

- Confirm that learning goals cover the full range of relevant learning opportunities and activities—academic as well as co-curricular.

- Communicate goals to students, colleagues in the institution, and other appropriate constituency groups.

2. Evaluate Learning Outcomes

- Develop appropriate learning outcome indicators, measures, and measurement procedures.

- Confirm that specific teaching and other instructional activities within the institution cover all of the defined goals, including general education goals, at increasing levels of difficulty and with effective coordination across the institution (e.g., assurance of appropriate coherence and avoidance of unnecessary duplication).

- Assess the extent to which established goals are being met with specific programs, services, and courses.

3. Use the Outcome Information

- Communicate results to colleagues in the institution and, as appropriate, to students and external constituents.

- Use outcomes information to improve teaching and learning in all programs and at all levels.

- Compare outcomes, as appropriate, with results from previous years and with those from peer, competitor, and/or leading institutions.

- Integrate results from student learning assessment with overall institutional assessment.

- Use the results to guide academic planning, resource allocation, and day-to-day decision making.

- Periodically review and, as appropriate, refine and update goals and the effectiveness of the processes involved in defining learning goals, evaluating outcomes, and using evaluative information for improvement.

EVIDENCE OF LEARNING

Studying outcomes requires the establishment of indicators and measures that operationalize program, department, and/or institutional teaching/learning goals into specific and concrete activities, actions, events, or occurrences for which appropriate evidence can be gathered—either by means of qualitative or quantitative analysis (Banta and Associates 2002; Banta 2004; Palomba and Banta 1999; Suskie 2004; Walvoord 2004). Ideally, an organization should base its assessment of learning outcomes on what are termed direct indicators of learning (National Communication Association 2006), but indirect and other indicators may also be helpful. See Figure 17 for examples of indicators that fall into each category.

FIGURE 17. INDICATORS OF LEARNING

Direct Indicators of Learning

- Entrance (pre) and exit (post) tests (course-specific & program-specific)
- Placement tests
- Portfolio assessment
- Capstone experiences (e.g., course, thesis, field project)
- Respected standardized tests and internally/externally-designed comprehensive (written and oral) exit tests and examinations;
- Senior thesis (multiple reviewers)
- Oral defense of senior thesis or project (multiple reviewers)
- Required oral presentations (multiple raters)
- National tests and examinations
- Performance on licensure, certification, or professional exams
- Essay questions (blind scored by multiple faculty)
- Required papers and research projects (multiple reviewers)
- Internal and external juried review of comprehensive senior projects
- Externally reviewed exhibits and performances
- External evaluation of internship performance

Indirect Indicators of Learning

- Exit interviews of graduates and focus groups
- Surveys of alumni, employers, and students
- Retention, persistence, graduation, and transfer rates and studies
- Length of time to degree (years/hours to completion)
- Grade distributions
- SAT scores
- Course enrollments and profiles
- Job placement data

Other Indicators of Learning

- Questionnaires asking students if their personal goals for course, major, or program have been met
- Instruments that collect data on indirect facts that can affect student success such as curriculum review reports or evaluation reports of program submitted by visiting committees of external peer experts (accreditation reports)
- Faculty publications and recognition
- Courses selected by majors, grades, and GPAs
- Faculty-student ratio
- Percentage of students who study abroad
- Enrollment trends
- Student diversity

In assessing learning outcomes in particular courses or competency areas, an organization should find it helpful to identify specific criteria or standards—sometimes called *rubrics* (e.g., Suskie 2004)—to use as foundations for both evaluation of individual course assignments and the broader evaluation of a course or academic program or service. To illustrate with a simple but familiar example, suppose that one goal of a particular course or program is to develop skills in written expression. In such an instance, the unit could develop standardized criteria to use in evaluating written assignments—which might include the following:

- Clarity of purpose or thesis
- Expression of a point of view
- Relevance of supportive information
- Use of examples and evidence
- Organization and clarity
- Grammar and punctuation
- Accuracy of references and reference style

The unit then could assign a particular number of points to, or create a rating scale for, each criterion. Individual assignments would be evaluated using the selected criteria and scoring system. Moreover, these scores could also be used in the aggregate, as one indicator of students' progress over the duration of the course or program. Ideally, longitudinal assessments of this kind would be done by a panel of evaluators, rather than by a single course instructor.

Each of the learning outcome indicators mentioned, and others that might be selected, has strengths and limitations, so a combination of methods is recommended. Through the selection and use of a number of measures, a unit can translate broad educational goals into specific, tangible, communicable, and measurable assessment standards to provide all involved with a clearer sense of how successful the institution, department, or program is in achieving its purposes. Proponents of learning outcomes assessment note also that clear goals and indicators help students understand expectations, motivate performance, make grading easier and faster, increase grading accuracy and consistency, minimize bias, improve communication, and diminish arguments over grades (Suskie 2004, 124–25).

FIGURE 18. SAMPLE DASHBOARD FOR AN ACADEMIC DEPARTMENT OR PROGRAM

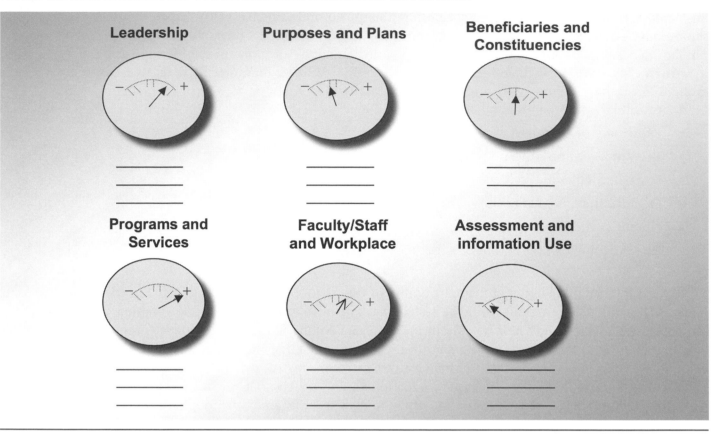

DASHBOARDS

Some programs, departments, and institutions take the step of identifying a small set of key indicators and measures—sometimes termed *dashboard indicators*—that they use to track outcomes and monitor progress in these critical areas, as illustrated in Figure 18. Dashboard indicators can be helpful in the same way that the gauges of an automobile's dashboard provide a quick reference to information on a vehicle's most important systems.

Regardless of the type of display method, the evidence used should be reliable, current, verifiable, coherent, objective, relevant, cumulative, representative, and actionable (Southern Association 2007; Western Association 2002, 10). The key is that whatever form assessment takes, the efforts must be "designed to provide relevant and trustworthy information to support institutional improvement" (New England Association 2004, 4).

COMPARISONS

As noted earlier, comparing outcomes and achievements over time to identify trends and patterns and to monitor progress is an important component of assessment. Another important type of comparison is with peers, leaders, and, where appropriate, competitor institutions or organizations.

Comparative assessment—also termed *benchmarking*—involves identifying, selecting, and systematically gathering information from other organizations in order to compare your organization's approaches and outcomes with theirs (Bender and Shuh 2002). The most obvious sources of comparisons are other institutions, departments, or programs within higher education. For example, national databases on alumni outcomes, student engagement, library holdings, funded research dollars generated, physical facilities, and IT resources can provide helpful information. In some instances, it is useful—or necessary—to create specialized benchmarking relationships with other institutions to get meaningful information for pertinent comparisons.

Depending on the unit, program, or service, opportunities sometimes also exist to draw comparisons with other industries that have comparable processes or activities. For example, instructional facilities or purchasing processes may be compared with similar processes in organizations in other sectors. In all cases, comparisons are an important tool for placing one's own outcomes information in a broader context.

THE BROAD PURPOSES OF ASSESSMENT

Most fundamentally, assessment is a means of monitoring the outcomes and achievements of an institution, department, or program to determine how well it is succeeding in fulfilling its purposes and plans, providing effective leadership, addressing the needs and expectations of internal and external beneficiaries and constituencies, developing and delivering high-quality programs and services, maintaining a high-quality and satisfying workplace for faculty and staff, and meaningfully assessing the results of efforts in those areas as a guide to continuous improvement. Assessment is viewed as "an essential part of the ongoing institutional self-study . . . to underline the necessity for each institution to formulate a plan which provides a series of outcomes measures that are internally consistent and in accord with its mission and structure" (Northwest Commission 2004, 9). Assessment is vital to an institution, for academic departments, and for student life, administrative, and service units. For each, the issue of determining and demonstrating its level of success in fulfilling its broad organizational goals, achieving its aspirations, and progressing in its plans is of vital importance.

6.0. ASSESSMENT AND INFORMATION USE: KEY REVIEW ISSUES

This category investigates how the institution, department, or program conducts assessment and how the assessment process is integrated into organizational life so that information on progress, outcomes, and achievements is used effectively to guide organizational decision making, resource allocation, planning, and improvement efforts. Specifically, Category 6 asks about how the institution, department, or program evaluates its accomplishments, progress, and standing relative to peers in the areas of leadership, purposes and plans, beneficiaries and constituencies, programs and services, faculty/staff and workplace, and assessment and information sharing. The category considers how evidence and measurement information is gathered and analyzed; how comparative information from peer, competitor, and leaders in the field is collected; and how that and other information is shared and used to assess and improve the institution, department, or program being reviewed.

AREAS TO ADDRESS

A. **Leadership Assessment**
  1. **How does the institution, department, or program assess the quality and effectiveness of its leadership and governance practices? (See discussion in Category 1.)**

  - What are the leadership and governance goals?

  - What sort of evidence—indicators or measures[2]—is used as the basis for assessing outcomes and progress toward those goals?

  - How were those indicators or measures established?

  - What information-gathering methods or procedures are employed?

  - How are assessment results communicated to colleagues within the institution and, as appropriate, to beneficiary and constituency groups?

  - How is outcomes information used to improve leadership practices, and the organization more generally?

  - How, and how often, are leadership assessment procedures—and approaches to using such information—reviewed and updated?

B. **Purposes and Plans Assessment**
  1. **How does the institution, department, or program assess its purposes and plans? (See discussion in Category 2.)**

  - What are the current goals in relation to your institution's, department's, or program's purposes and plans?

  - What sort of evidence—indicators or measures[3]—is used as the basis for assessing outcomes and progress toward those goals?

  - How were those indicators or measures established?

  - What information-gathering methods and procedures are employed?

  - How are assessment results communicated to colleagues within the institution and, as appropriate, to beneficiary and constituency groups?

  - How is outcomes information used to advance the organization's purposes and plans, and those of the institution more generally?

  - How, and how often, are these assessment procedures—and approaches to using this information—reviewed and updated?

C. **Beneficiaries and Constituencies Assessment**
  1. **How does the organization assess its effectiveness in learning about student and/or other beneficiary and constituency group needs, expectations, and experiences, and in using this information to establish mutually beneficial and satisfying relationships? (See discussion in Category 3.)**

  - What are your primary goals related to each of your beneficiary and constituency groups?

  - What sort of evidence—indicators or measures[4]—is used as the basis for assessing outcomes and progress toward those goals?

- How were those indicators or measures established?

- What information-gathering methods and procedures are employed?

- How are assessment results communicated to colleagues within the institution and, as appropriate, to other groups?

- How is outcomes information used to improve beneficiary and constituency group relationships, and the organization more generally?

- How, and how often, are these assessment procedures—and approaches to using this information—reviewed and updated?

D. Programs and Services Assessment

1. Mission-Critical Programs and Services and Associated Processes

How does the institution, department, or program assess mission-critical programs, services, and associated processes? (See discussion in Category 4.)

- What are the primary goals of each of your mission-critical programs and services?

- For each program or service, what are your goals for the most important associated processes?

- What sort of evidence—indicators or measures—is used to assess outcomes and progress related to your mission-critical program, service, and process goals?

- How were those indicators and measures[5] established?

- What information-gathering methods and procedures are employed?

- How are assessment results communicated to colleagues within the institution and, as appropriate, to other groups?

- How is outcomes information used to improve mission-critical programs, services, and processes, and the organization more generally?

- How, and how often, are assessment procedures—and approaches to using this information—reviewed and updated?

2. Operational and Support Services and Associated Processes

How does the institution, department, or program assess the effectiveness and efficiency of important operational and support services and associated processes? (See discussion in Category 4.2.)

- What are your primary goals in relation to operational and support services?

- What sort of evidence—indicators or measures—is used as the basis for assessment?

- How were those indicators or measures[6] established?

- What information-gathering methods and procedures are employed?

- How is outcomes information used to improve operational and support programs, services, and processes, and the organization more generally?

- How are assessment results communicated to colleagues and, as appropriate, others within the institution?

- How is outcomes information used to improve operational and support services, associated processes, and the organization more generally?

- How, and how often, are assessment procedures—and approaches to using this information—reviewed and updated?

E. **Faculty/Staff and Workplace Assessment**
   1. **How does the institution, department, or program assess its effectiveness in establishing a positive workplace—understanding and addressing faculty and staff needs and evaluating faculty/staff satisfaction and workplace climate? (See discussion in Category 5.)**
   - What are your faculty/staff and workplace goals?
   - What sort of evidence—indicators or measures—is used as the basis for assessment?
   - How were those indicators or measures[7] established?
   - What information-gathering methods and procedures are employed?
   - How are assessment results communicated to colleagues within the institution and to other groups as appropriate?
   - How is outcomes information used to improve faculty and staff satisfaction, workplace climate, and the organization more generally?
   - How, and how often, are assessment procedures—and approaches to using this information—reviewed and updated?

F. **Assessment and Information Use Assessment**
   1. **How does the institution, department, or program evaluate the effectiveness of its approaches to assessment and the sharing and using of information and expertise?**
   - What are your goals relative to assessment and information sharing?
   - What sort of evidence—indicators or measures—is used as the basis for assessment?
   - How were those indicators or measures[8] established?
   - What information-gathering methods and procedures are employed?
   - How are assessment results communicated to colleagues within the institution and others as appropriate?
   - How is outcomes information used to improve assessment and information sharing and use, and the organization more generally?
   - How, and how often, are assessment procedures—and approaches to sharing and using this information—reviewed and updated?

6.2. COMPARATIVE ANALYSIS[9]

AREAS TO ADDRESS

1. **For EHE categories 1 through 6, how does your institution, department, or program compare current outcomes with results from previous years?**

2. **For each EHE category, what institutions, departments, and/or programs have been selected for comparative analysis, and why were they selected?**

3. How does your institution, department, or program use comparative information from peers, competitors, and/or leaders in the field to interpret its own outcomes and achievements?

4. How does the organization keep its methods for gathering comparison information up to date with current and future institution, department, or program needs?

6.3. INFORMATION SHARING AND USE

AREAS TO ADDRESS

A. Availability and Dissemination
   1. How are data and information collected, stored, retrieved, and disseminated to ensure availability to and access by appropriate people and departments?

   2. What organizational information, including assessment results, is regularly communicated to internal and external groups? When and how does that take place?
   - How does the organization determine which data and information to collect, store, and disseminate?
   - How are the accessibility and usability of your information and information systems ensured?
   - How are the integrity, reliability, accuracy, timeliness, and security of data and information ensured?
   - How does the organization keep software and hardware systems current with educational and/or administrative needs and directions?

   3. How does your organization address information and information technology policy issues, including:
   - Access?
   - Privacy and confidentiality?
   - Authoritativeness?
   - Internet use?
   - Proprietary rights?
   - Security?

B. Information and Knowledge Utilization
   1. How does the institution, department, and/or program encourage and reward the sharing and use of knowledge resources and expertise among people within your organization?

   2. How does the organization ensure that information reaches appropriate individuals, groups, and organizations?

3. How does the organization determine whether the available types, forms, and formats of data and information are appropriate for addressing user needs?

NOTES

1. The author gratefully acknowledges the influence of the Middle States Commission on Higher Education (2002, 2003a, 2003b) publications and discussions with Jean Avnet Morse in the development of this general model of assessment planning presented in Figure 12, and the learning outcomes assessment model described in Figure 16.

2. Various indicators, measures, and other sources of evidence can be used for assessing outcomes, including trend data, survey data, comparisons, satisfaction indices, national norms on student learning or other outcomes, accreditation or review results, or focus group findings (Southern Association 2006).

   In assessing the effectiveness of leadership and governance, evidence might include the implementation of new leadership feedback systems, improvements in leadership or leadership practices based on performance reviews or feedback, changes in organizational climate attributed to leadership initiatives, measures of leadership engagement, and service in leadership roles in external campus, public, or professional groups and organizations. See discussion in Category 1.

3. Various indicators, measures, and other sources of evidence can be used for assessing the effectiveness of strategic planning, including progress on annual goals, benefits of a new planning process, improvements in the way goals and plans are established and measured, measures of faculty/staff engagement in the planning process, coordination of plans across departments or work groups, and indicators of the effectiveness of dissemination of information regarding plans. See Figure 14 and discussion in Category 2.

4. Indicators of the quality and effectiveness of relationships with beneficiary and constituency groups might include satisfaction/dissatisfaction results from mail or phone surveys, focus groups, interviews, information from advisory groups, suggestion box responses, reports from "mystery shoppers," and analysis of complaints and commendations. Also potentially useful, depending on the organization and the external groups involved, are indirect measures such as attrition rates, recommendations and referrals, invitations and requests to serve in leadership roles in external groups, enrollment demand and trends, results of course/instructor evaluations, complaint or suggestion content and rate, financial support, or publication acceptance rates. The appropriateness of methods will vary from organization to organization and group to group. Note: While it may be impossible to implement systematic assessment methods for all constituency groups, the presumption is that indicators and appropriate methods should be in place for all priority beneficiary and constituency groups. See Figure 14, and discussion in Category 3.

5. For academic programs and services, indicators include direct evidence of learning such as pre- and post-course/curriculum results, certification and licensure rates, and analysis of student portfolios, or the extent to which needs and expectations have been met, overall satisfaction, and the quality and effectiveness of instruction, scholarship, and outreach. If the goal is to evaluate an academic unit more broadly, indicators might also include departmental distinctions or recognition, program ratings or rankings, retention

rates, faculty/staff accomplishments, number of applicants or majors, applicant scores on standardized tests, time-to-degree, enrollment or resource generation, faculty publications, leadership in external groups and organizations, research and grants activity, publications, outreach activity levels, productivity or cost-effectiveness outcomes, and other measures selected as appropriate. See Figure 17. See also discussion in Category 4.1.

For administrative, student life, and service departments, outcome and achievement indicators might include measures of student learning and satisfaction, and also of effectiveness, efficiency, value, or innovativeness of programs and services, and other indicators of success in fulfilling the unit's purposes, aspirations, and broad organizational goals. See Figure 14, and discussion in Category 4.1.

6. For operational and support services, indicators might include outcomes and achievements in areas that are largely invisible to external groups but essential to the effectiveness and efficiency of mission-critical programs and services and the functioning of the organization, more generally. Accomplishments that relate to the operational support of instruction, for instance, would include scheduling, staffing, evaluation, purchasing, budgeting, employee recruitment and hiring, training and professional development, information management, e-mail and telephone systems, and logistical support of all types. Note that in some administrative organizations, the preceding processes listed as examples of organizational support processes may be mission-critical processes. For instance, in a human resources department, the work of a professional development office is likely to be regarded as mission critical. See Figure 14, and discussion in Category 4.2.

7. Indicators of faculty/staff satisfaction and workplace climate might include the results of satisfaction or climate surveys or interviews, retention or turnover rates, absenteeism, analysis of exit interviews, or other indicators selected by the unit. See Figure 14, and discussion in Category 5.

8. Evidence of outcomes and achievements in the area of assessment and information sharing might include documented improvements in performance measurement methods, advances in approaches to gathering and using comparison information from other organizations, measures of the effectiveness and/or efficiency of information dissemination and use, dissemination and adoption of "best practices," or improvements in information and information systems access, reliability, effectiveness, or security. See Figure 14, and discussion in Category 6.

9. *Comparative assessment*—also termed *benchmarking*—refers to the process of identifying, selecting, and systematically gathering information from other organizations in order to compare your organization's performance, programs, services, processes, activities, achievements, and/or impact with those of other organizations. Comparisons may be with peer and/or competitor higher education institutions or organizations in other industries that have processes or activities comparable to those of your unit. For example, instructional, facilities, or purchasing processes may be compared with similar processes at peer or competitor colleges or universities or organizations in other sectors. Comparisons with recognized leaders in higher education and/or leaders in business, health care, or governmental organizations can provide a basis for setting more ambitious goals for your own organization.

7.0

OUTCOMES AND ACHIEVEMENTS

For any college or university, as well as for the academic, student life, administrative, or service programs or departments it comprises, effectiveness and quality are the ultimate aims. Realizing those aims involves achieving and sustaining high standards relative to leadership, purposes and plans, beneficiary and constituency relationships, programs and services, faculty/staff satisfaction and a positive workplace climate, and assessment and information use practices. It entails having the information and evidence available to determine, document, and/or demonstrate outcomes and achievements in an objective manner for the benefit of the organization itself and for other constituencies.

Whereas Category 6 is concerned with establishing an assessment system that permits the gathering and use of the information and evidence necessary to accomplish that goal, Category 7 focuses on the results obtained from the assessment process. Questions in this category relate to documented achievements and outcomes relative to the each of the six EHE categories.

7.0. OUTCOMES AND ACHIEVEMENTS: KEY REVIEW ISSUES

Category 7 investigates outcomes and trends. To place such excellence outcomes and achievements in the most meaningful context, the results of comparisons are also a topic of consideration. Comparisons allow an institution, department, or program to relate its accomplishments in the areas of leadership, purposes and plans, beneficiary and constituency relationships, programs and services, faculty/staff and workplace climate, and assessment and information sharing to those of other organizations. Figures 19 through 25 provide illustrative charts one can use to organize and present this kind of information.

In summary, then, this category asks for the kind of information and evidence that allows an institution, department, or program to determine and/or demonstrate where it stands now, over time, and in comparison to peers, competitors, and/or leaders for each of the EHE categories 1 through 6. See Figure 26.

FIGURE 19. LEADERSHIP

7.1 Leadership

Indicators (What We Currently Assess)	Outcomes For This Year (+/-/?)	Compared to Previous Years (+/-/Flat/?)	Compared to Plans and Goals (+/-/Flat/?)	Compared to Peers and Leaders (+/-/Flat/?)
•				
•				
•				
•				
•				
•				
•				
•				

FIGURE 20. PURPOSES AND PLANS

7.2 Purposes and Plans

Indicators (What We Currently Assess)	Outcomes For This Year (+/-/?)	Compared to Previous Years (+/-/Flat/?)	Compared to Plans and Goals (+/-/Flat/?)	Compared to Peers and Leaders (+/-/Flat/?)
•				
•				
•				
•				
•				
•				
•				
•				

FIGURE 21. BENEFICIARIES AND CONSTITUENCIES

7.3 Beneficiaries and Constituencies

Indicators for Each Group (What We Currently Assess)	Outcomes For This Year (+/-/?)	Compared to Previous Years (+/-/Flat/?)	Compared to Plans and Goals (+/-/Flat/?)	Compared to Peers and Leaders (+/-/Flat/?)
•				
•				
•				
•				
•				
•				
•				
•				

FIGURE 22. PROGRAMS AND SERVICES (MISSION-CRITICAL)

7.4A Programs and Services (Mission-Critical)

Indicators for Each Program/Service (What We Currently Assess)	Outcomes For This Year (+/-/?)	Compared to Previous Years (+/-/Flat/?)	Compared to Plans and Goals (+/-/Flat/?)	Compared to Peers and Leaders (+/-/Flat/?)
•				
•				
•				
•				
•				
•				
•				
•				

FIGURE 23. SERVICES (OPERATIONAL AND SUPPORT SERVICES)

7.4B Services (Operational and Support Services)

Indicators (What We Currently Assess)	Outcomes For This Year (+/-/?)	Compared to Previous Years (+/-/Flat/?)	Compared to Plans and Goals (+/-/Flat/?)	Compared to Peers and Leaders (+/-/Flat/?)
•				
•				
•				
•				
•				
•				
•				
•				

FIGURE 24. FACULTY/STAFF AND WORKPLACE

7.5 Faculty/Staff and Workplace

Indicators for Each Group (What We Currently Assess)	Outcomes For This Year (+/-/?)	Compared to Previous Years (+/-/Flat/?)	Compared to Plans and Goals (+/-/Flat/?)	Compared to Peers and Leaders (+/-/Flat/?)
•				
•				
•				
•				
•				
•				
•				
•				

FIGURE 25. ASSESSMENT AND INFORMATION USE

7.6 Assessment and Information Use

Indicators (What We Currently Assess)	Outcomes For This Year (+/-/?)	Compared to Previous Years (+/-/Flat/?)	Compared to Plans and Goals (+/-/Flat/?)	Compared to Peers and Leaders (+/-/Flat/?)
·				
·				
·				
·				
·				
·				
·				
·				

FIGURE 26. SAMPLE EXCELLENCE LEVELS AND TRENDS PERFORMANCE CHART

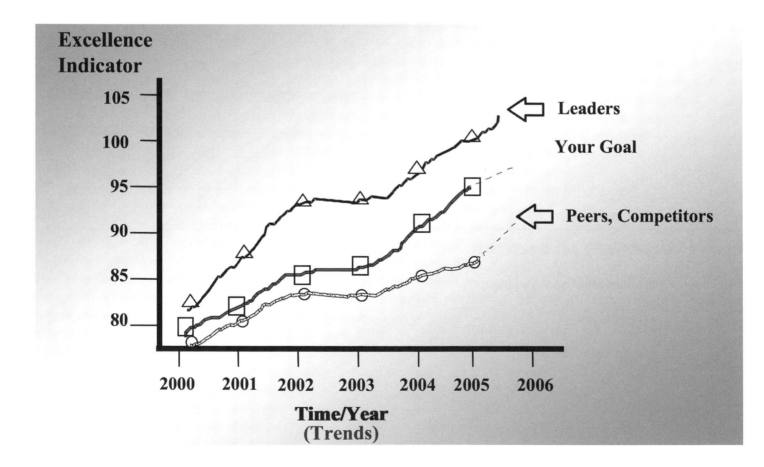

7.1. LEADERSHIP

AREAS TO ADDRESS

1. What are the current and over-time outcomes and achievements related to leadership and governance effectiveness?[1]

2. How do those outcomes and achievements compare with those of peers, competitors, and/or leaders in the institution or field?[2]

7.2. PURPOSES AND PLANS

AREAS TO ADDRESS

1. What are the current and over-time outcomes and achievements related to your purposes and plans?

2. How do those outcomes and achievements compare with those of peers, competitors, and/or leaders?

7.3. BENEFICIARIES AND CONSTITUENCIES

AREAS TO ADDRESS

1. What are the documented outcomes and achievements related to your relationships with beneficiary and constituency groups?

2. How do those outcomes and achievements compare with those of peers, competitors, and/or leaders?

7.4. PROGRAMS AND SERVICES

AREAS TO ADDRESS

A. Mission-Critical Programs, Services, and Associated Processes
   1. What are the current and over-time outcomes and achievements related to mission-critical programs and services—and their associated processes?

   2. How do those outcomes and achievements compare with those of peers, competitors, and/or leaders?

B. Operational and Support Services and Associated Processes
   1. What are the current and over-time outcomes and achievements related to the effectiveness and efficiency of important operational and support services—and their associated processes?

2. How do those outcomes and achievements compare with those of peers, competitors, and/or leaders?

7.5. FACULTY/STAFF SATISFACTION AND WORKPLACE CLIMATE

AREAS TO ADDRESS

1. What are the current and over-time outcomes and achievements related to faculty and staff satisfaction and workplace climate?

2. How do those outcomes and achievements compare with those of peers, competitors, and/or leaders?

7.6. ASSESSMENT AND INFORMATION USE

AREAS TO ADDRESS

1. What are the current and over-time outcomes and achievements related to the effectiveness of assessment and information-sharing approaches, methods, and practices?

2. How do those outcomes and achievements compare with those of peers, competitors, and/or leaders?

NOTES

1. This category assesses results and evidence that document outcomes and achievements. The category does not consider information on the organization's approaches, intentions, strategies, or methods. Those topics are the focus of categories 1 through 6. Wherever possible, outcomes, achievements, progress (trends), and comparisons should be presented in graphs and tables that display results in a clear and unambiguous manner.

   Outcomes and achievements related to each category should be based on established measures and indicators, as discussed in Category 6.

2. Comparisons relate your outcomes and achievements in each category to those of peers, competitors, and/or leaders, as discussed in Category 6. Wherever possible, comparison information should be presented in graphs and tables that display results in a clear and unambiguous manner.

GLOSSARY

achievements. Tangible evidence of results, accomplishments, or outcomes.

action plans. Specific activities and steps taken as a part of short- and long-term strategic planning. Through action plan development, general strategies and goals are made specific so that effective implementation is possible and probable.

alignment. Consistency and synchronization of plans, processes, actions, information, and decisions among units to support key unit- and institution-wide goals. Effective alignment requires a shared understanding of purposes and goals and the use of complementary measures and information to enable planning, tracking, analysis, and improvement at the institutional, departmental, work group, and individual level.

approach. The methods and strategies used by an organization. Categories 1 through 6 focus on approach along with implementation.

assessment. A process of reviewing the approaches, implementation strategies, and outcomes of an institution, department, or program. In this sense, the entire Excellence in Higher Education model is an assessment framework. More specifically, assessment refers to the process of comparing achievements and outcomes against a set of goals in order to evaluate progress and guide further improvement efforts. This narrower sense of the term is the focus in Category 6.

benchmarking. Establishing benchmarks—also termed comparisons—refers to the process of identifying, selecting, and systematically comparing the organization's performance, activities, programs, services, processes, achievements, and/or impact with those of other organizations. Comparisons may be with peer, competitor, and/or leading institutions or with organizations in other sectors with similar processes or activities.

beneficiaries. Stakeholders, consumers, clients, publics, users, constituencies, or "customers" for whom the organization undertakes activities or provides programs or services. Depending on the mission of the organization, such services may include instruction, scholarship, public service/outreach, and administrative, support, or other functions. The list of beneficiaries may include students, faculty, staff, disciplinary and professional communities, potential employers, alumni, academic associations, parents, business and industry, state and federal funding agencies, private foundations and donors, prospective students and parents, graduate and professional schools, advisory boards, disciplinary and administrative opinion leaders at other institutions, local and state government, the citizens of the community or state, and other groups. For administrative departments that provide programs and services within the institution—such as departments of human resources, facilities, computing services, and sponsored research; faculty/administrative councils or assemblies; and other administrative and service units—the relevant internal administrative and academic departments are those served by, influencing, or influenced by the unit. Also included are units inside or outside the institution with which the institution, department, or program collaborates.

collaborators. External groups or organizations with which the unit must coordinate to carry out its mission-critical work. Includes partnerships, alliances, and vendor-supplier relationships.

comparisons. Establishing comparisons—also termed benchmarking—refers to the process of identifying, selecting, and systematically comparing the organization's performance, programs, services, processes, activities, achievements, and/or impact with those of other organizations. Comparisons may be with peer, competitor, and/or leading institutions or with organizations in other sectors with comparable processes or activities.

coordination. Alignment and synchronization of plans, processes, actions, information, and decisions throughout an institution, department, or program. Effective coordination requires common understanding of purposes and goals and the use of complementary measures and information to enable planning, tracking, analysis, and improvement at the institutional, unit, work group, and individual level.

cycle time. The time required to fulfill commitments or to complete tasks.

dashboard performance indicators. A set of performance measures or indicators—sometimes referred to as a scorecard—that summarizes and displays results for areas of organizational functions identified as essential to assessing organizational excellence.

effectiveness. Success in achieving an intended purpose.

efficiency. Economies relative to time, dollars, and resources.

faculty/staff. Refers to all faculty and staff groups. This includes full- and part-time faculty, teaching assistants, full- and part-time staff, and student workers.

goals. High-level targets or end points that are sufficiently specific to allow for progress to be assessed and a determination to be made when they have been achieved.

groups and organizations served. Beneficiaries, stakeholders, consumers, clients, publics, users, constituencies, or "customers" for which the organization undertakes activities or provides programs or services, or with which it collaborates. Depending on the mission of the organization, the services may include instruction, scholarship, public service/outreach, and administrative, support, or other functions. The list of groups and organizations may include students, faculty, staff, disciplinary and professional communities, potential employers, alumni, academic associations, parents, business and industry, state and federal funding agencies, private foundations and donors, prospective students and parents, graduate and professional schools, advisory boards, disciplinary and administrative opinion leaders at other institutions, local and state government, the citizens of the community or state, and other groups. For administrative departments that provide programs and services within the institution—such as departments of human resources, facilities, computing services, and sponsored research; faculty/administrative councils or assemblies; and other administrative and service units—the relevant groups and organizations are the administrative and academic departments that are served by, influence, or are influenced by the unit. The phrase also refers to departments inside or outside the institution with which the institution, department, or program collaborates.

implementation. The manner in which approaches are deployed and applied within the organization.

knowledge utilization. Effective dissemination, sharing, and use of information, expertise, and knowledge by members of an organization.

leadership system. The exercise of leadership and governance, formally and informally, throughout the organization; the way decisions are made, communicated, and carried out. The concept includes structures and mechanisms for decision making, leader selection, and the development of leaders.

measures. Measures or indicators identified by a unit as appropriate for assessing, documenting, or monitoring organizational outcomes and achievement levels. Measures include indicators of achievement relative to the mission, vision, values, goals, and plans and the quality, effectiveness, and efficiency of leadership practices, planning processes, relationships with the beneficiary and constituency groups and organizations, programs and services, faculty/staff and workplace climate, and assessment and information use approaches.

mission. The primary work of the unit; the purposes for which the unit exists, including specification of the groups for which programs or services are provided. Often published and made available to members of the organization and beyond.

mission-critical programs, services, and processes. The most fundamental activities and associated sequences of work activities performed by an institution, department, or program. Also termed core programs, services, and processes, these are the activities about which the organization has particular expertise. For academic units, mission-critical work processes typically include activities directly associated with teaching/learning, scholarship, and service/outreach. In administrative organizations, core processes vary substantially from department to department, reflecting in each case the unique mission, activities, programs, and services.

organization. Used in a general sense to refer to an entire institution, an administrative or academic program or department, a service or administrative department, a faculty assembly, or a senate—any structured work unit within a higher education context.

outcomes. The organization's current accomplishments and achievements and performance over time relative to its purposes and plans, leadership practices, relationships with the beneficiary and constituency groups and organizations, programs and services, faculty/staff and workplace climate, and assessment and information use approaches.

overview. Summary of an organization's major programs and services, structure, key relationships, major recommendations from previous external or internal assessments, key challenges and opportunities, peers and/or competitors, and other information important to understanding the context in which the organization operates. The information is assembled as a part of the preparation for an assessment.

performance. Refers to output and results. Performance information permits evaluation relative to goals, standards, past results, and the accomplishments of peer and other organizations.

process. A sequence of activities. Processes include combinations of people, machines, tools, techniques, and materials in a systematic series of steps, actions, or activities with a specified beginning and end.

recognition. Methods for acknowledging the contributions of individuals, groups, or work units. It includes but is not limited to public acknowledgment of individuals and groups or teams, personal feedback, and merit awards. Also included are letters of commendation, certifications of merit, articles in bulletins or newsletters, announcements at unit meetings.

results. The outcomes and achievements of an institution, department, or program.

service standards. Organizational practices implemented to address identified needs and expectations of groups being served. They apply to those processes and people with direct contact with those external groups. Examples might include standards regarding callback response time, response time to inquiries, wait times, or telephone-answering protocol.

stakeholders. Sometimes termed beneficiaries, external groups, consumers, clients, publics, users, constituencies, or "customers," stakeholders are those persons or groups who are served by, influence, or are influenced by the organization. They include those whose assessments are critical to the support and reputation of the organization. The list may include students, parents/family, faculty, staff, disciplinary and professional communities, potential employers, alumni, academic associations, business and industry, state and federal funding agencies, private foundations and donors, prospective students and parents, graduate and professional schools, disciplinary and administrative opinion leaders at other institutions, local and state government, citizens of the community or state, and others.

suppliers and collaborators. Groups or organizations with which an organization collaborates that provide capital, material, or human resources necessary for an institution, department, or program to fulfill its mission. Alliance, partner, and supplier relationships may exist with other departments in the institution such as admissions, scheduling, human resources, or accounting. They may also exist with organizations outside the institution, such as high schools, community and junior colleges, and other colleges or universities. Other examples are vendors of various types that supply goods and services.

support services. Sequences of activities necessary to the completion of mission-critical work and to the effective and efficient operation of the organization. Often such processes are invisible to external groups. For example, organizational processes would include recruiting and hiring, conducting performance reviews, preparing budgets, training, purchasing equipment and supplies, coordinating repairs and maintenance, time and room scheduling, preparing work materials, and scheduling and conducting meetings.

synchronization. Alignment and coordination of plans, processes, actions, information, and decisions throughout an institution, department, or program. Effective synchronization requires a shared understanding of purposes and goals and use of complementary measures and information to enable planning, tracking, analysis, and improvement at the institutional, unit, work group, and individual level.

vision. A characterization of how the institution, department, or program sees itself in the future; its broadly expressed aspirations.

WORKS CITED AND
SUGGESTED READINGS

Academic Quality Improvement Program (AQIP). The Higher Learning Commission. 2005. *Principles and Categories for Improving Academic Quality.* The Higher Learning Commission. http://www.aqip.org/index. php?option=com_docman&task=doc_view&gid=38&Itemid=128>.

Ahmed, A. M., J. B. Yang, and B. G. Dale. 2003. "Self-Assessment Methodology: The Route to Business Excellence." *Quality Management Journal* 10(1): 43–58.

Albrighton, F., and J. Thomas. 2001. *Managing External Relations.* Buckingham, U.K.: Open University Press.

Aldridge, S., and J. Rowley. 1998. "Measuring Customer Satisfaction in Higher Education." *Quality Assurance in Education* 6(4): 197–204.

Andersen, B., and T. Fagerhaug. 2001. *Performance Measurement Explained: Designing and Implementing Your State-of-the-Art System.* Milwaukee: American Society for Quality.

Andrade, S. 1999. "How to Institutionalize Strategic Planning." *Planning for Higher Education* 27(1): 40–54.

Ashkenas, R., D. Ulrich, T. Jick, and S. Kerr. 2002. *The Boundaryless Organization.* San Francisco: Jossey-Bass.

Association of American Colleges and Universities. 2002. *Greater Expectations: A New Vision for Learning as a Nation Goes to College.* Washington, D.C.: Association of American Colleges and Universities.

Association of American Colleges and Universities. 2004. *Taking Responsibility for the Quality of the Baccalaureate Degree.* Washington, D.C.: Association of American Colleges and Universities.

Astin, A. W. 1991. *Assessing for Excellence: The Philosophy and Practice of Evaluation and Assessment in Higher Education.* Phoenix: Oryx Press.

Astin, A. W., and H. S. Astin. 2000. *Leadership Reconsidered: Engaging Higher Education in Social Change.* Battle Creek, Mich.: W. K. Kellogg Foundation.

Baenninger, M. A., and J. A. Morse. 2004. "Accrediting Learning." *In Contexts for Learning,* edited by B. Keith, 213–41. Stillwater, Okla.: New Forums Press.

Balderston, F. 1995. *Managing Today's University: Strategies for Viability, Change, and Excellence.* 2nd ed. San Francisco: Jossey-Bass.

Baldrige National Quality Program. 2007a. *The 2007 Criteria for Performance Excellence in Business.* Washington, D.C.: National Institute of Standards and Technology. <www.quality.nist.gov/Business_Criteria.htm>.

Baldrige National Quality Program. 2007b. *The 2007 Criteria for Performance Excellence in Education.* Washington, D.C.: National Institute of Standards and Technology. <www.quality.nist.gov/Education_Criteria.htm>.

Baldrige National Quality Program. 2007. Program Web site on the National Institute of Standards and Technology Web pages. <www.quality.nist.gov>.

Banta, T. W. 1993. *Making a Difference: Outcomes of a Decade of Assessment in Higher Education.* San Francisco: Jossey-Bass.

Banta, T. W. 2003. *Portfolio Assessment: Uses, Cases, Scoring, and Impact.* San Francisco: Wiley.

Banta, T. W. 2004. *Portfolio Assessment: Uses, Cases, Scoring, and Impact: Assessment Update Collection.* San Francisco: Jossey-Bass.

Banta, T. W., and associates. 2002. *Building a Scholarship of Assessment.* San Francisco: Jossey-Bass.

Bender, B. E., and J. H. Schuh, eds. 2002. *Using Benchmarking to Inform Practice in Higher Education.* New Directions for Higher Education, no. 118. San Francisco: Jossey-Bass.

Bennis, W. 1997. *Managing People Is Like Herding Cats.* Provo, Utah: Executive Excellence Publishing.

Bernstein, D., A. N. Burnett, A. Goodburn, and P. Savory. 2006. *Making Teaching and Learning Visible: Course Portfolios and the Peer Review of Teaching.* Bolton, Mass.: Anker.

Birnbaum, R., and J. Deshotels. 1999. "Has the Academy Adopted TQM?" *Planning for Higher Education* 28(1): 29–37.

Blair, D. C. 2002. "Knowledge Management: Hype, Hope, or Help?" *Journal of the American Society for Information Science and Technology* 53(12): 1019–28.

Blazey, M. L. 2003. *Insights to Performance Excellence 2003: An Inside Look at the 2003 Baldrige Award Criteria.* Milwaukee: American Society for Quality.

Boatman, S. A. 1999. "The Leadership Audit: A Process to Enhance the Development of Student Leadership." *NASPA Journal* 37(1): 325–36.

Bogue, E. G., and K. B. Hall. 2003. *Quality and Accountability in Higher Education: Improving Policy, Enhancing Performance.* Westport, Conn.: Praeger.

Bowen, W. G., and H. T. Shapiro, eds. 1998. *Universities and Their Leadership.* Princeton, N.J.: Princeton University Press.

Brancato, C. K. 1995. *New Corporate Performance Measures.* New York: The Conference Board.

Brennan, J., and T. Shah. 2002. *Managing Quality in Higher Education: An International Perspective on Institutional Assessment and Change.* Buckingham, U.K.: OECD, SRHE, and Open University Press.

Bresciani, Marilee J. 2006. *Outcomes-Based Academic and Co-Curricular Program Review.* Sterling, Va.: Stylus.

Bryson, J. M. 1995. *Strategic Planning for Public and Nonprofit Organizations.* Rev. ed. San Francisco: Jossey-Bass.

Bryson, J. M., and F. K. Alston. 1996. *Creating and Implementing Your Own Strategic Plan: A Workbook for Public and Nonprofit Organizations.* San Francisco: Jossey-Bass.

Burke, J. C. 1997. *Performance-Funding Indicators: Concerns, Values, and Models for Two- and Four-Year Colleges and Universities.* Albany, N.Y.: Nelson A. Rockefeller Institute of Government.

Burkhardt, J. C. 2002. "Boundary-Spanning Leadership in Higher Education." *Journal of Leadership Studies* 8(3): 145–50.

Calhoun, J. M. 2002. *Using the Baldrige Criteria to Manage and Assess the Performance of Your Organization. Journal for Quality and Participation* 25(2): 45–53.

Camp, R. C. 1995. *Business Process Benchmarking: Finding and Implementing Best Practices.* Milwaukee: American Society for Quality Press.

Canic, M. J., and P. M. McCarthy. 2000. "Service Quality and Higher Education Do Mix." *Quality Management Forum* 33(9): 41–48.

"Changing the Way Student Professional Data Is Stored and Shared." 2004. Berkeley: University of California–Berkeley. <http://bearlink.berkeley.edu/ePortfolio/>.

Cheng, Y. C. 2003. "Quality Assurance in Education: Internal, Interface, and Future." *Quality Assurance in Education* 11(4): 202–13.

Cheng, Y. C., and W. M. Tam. 1997. "Multi-Models of Quality in Education." *Quality Assurance in Education* 5(1): 22–31.

Collins, J. C. 2001. *Good to Great.* New York: HarperCollins.

Collins, J. C., and J. I. Porras. 1994. *Built to Last.* New York: HarperCollins.

Consortium for Research on Emotional Intelligence in Organizations. 2005. <www.EIConsortium.org>.

Cooper, R. K., and A. Sawaf. 1997. *Executive EQ: Emotional Intelligence in Leadership and Organizations.* New York: Penguin Putnam.

Council for Higher Education Accreditation (CHEA). 2007. Washington, D.C. <www.chea.org/>.

Council for the Advancement of Standards in Higher Education. 2007. <www.cas.edu/>.

Covey, S. R. 1991. *Principle-Centered Leadership.* New York: Fireside.

Cruickshank, M. 2003. "Total Quality Management in the Higher Education Sector: A Literature Review from an International Sector and Australian Perspective." *Total Quality Management and Business Excellence* 14(10): 1159–67.

Cullen, J., J. Joyce, T. Hassell, and M. Broadbent. 2003. "Quality in Higher Education: From Monitoring to Management." *Quality Assurance in Education* 11(1): 5–14.

Curkovic, S., D. Menyk, R. Calantone, and R. Handfield. 2000. "Validating the Malcolm Baldrige National Quality Award Framework through Structural Equation Modeling." *International Journal of Production Research* 38(4): 765–91.

Daniels, S. E., and M. R. Hagen. 1999. "Making the Pitch in the Executive Suite." *Quality Progress* 32(4): 25–33.

Davenport, T. H., L. Prusak, and H. J. Wilson. 2003. "Who's Bringing You Hot Ideas (and How Are You Responding)?" *Harvard Business Review,* February, pp. 3–8.

Detomasi, D. 1995. "Mission Statements: One More Time." *Planning for Higher Education* 24(1): 31–35.

Dill, D. D., and C. P. Friedman. 1979. "An Analysis of Frameworks for Research on Innovation and Change in Higher Education." *Review of Educational Research* 49(3): 411–35.

Dodd, A. H. 2004a. "Accreditation as a Catalyst for Institutional Effectiveness." *New Directions for Institutional Research,* no. 123: 13.

Dodd, A. H. 2004b. "Conflict Communication and the Use of Quality Management Practices in Academic Departments." Paper presented at National Consortium for Continuous Improvement in Higher Education Annual Conference, July, Milwaukee.

Doerfel, M. L., and B. D. Ruben. 2002. "Developing More Adaptive, Innovative, and Interactive Organizations." In *Using Benchmarking to Inform Practice in Higher Education,* edited by B. E. Bender and J. H. Schuh. New Directions in Higher Education, no. 118. San Francisco: Jossey-Bass.

Dooris, M. J., J. M. Kelley, and J. F. Trainer, issue eds. 2004. "Successful Strategic Planning" (issue title). *New Directions for Institutional Research,* no. 123.

Douglas, T., and L. Fredenhall. 2004. "Evaluating the Deming Management Model of Total Quality in Services." *Decision Sciences* 35(3): 393–422.

Dressel, P. L. 1981. *Administrative Leadership: Effective and Responsive Decision Making in Higher Education.* San Francisco: Jossey-Bass.

Drew, J. R., and M. M. Nearing. 2004. *Continuous Quality Improvement in Higher Education.* Westport, Conn.: Praeger.

Driscoll, A., and D. Cordero de Noriega. 2006. *Taking Ownership of Accreditation: Assessment Processes That Promote Institutional Improvement and Faculty Engagement.* Sterling, Va.: Stylus

Eaton, J. S. 2005a. "Accreditation and the Chief Business Officer/Chief Financial Officer." Paper presented at Annual Conference of the National Association of College and University Business Officers, Baltimore, July 2005.

Eaton, J. S. 2006. "An Overview of U.S. Accreditation." Council for Higher Education Accreditation, Washington, D.C. <www.chea.org/pdf/OverviewAccred_rev0706.pdf>.

Eckel, P., M. Green, and B. Hill. 2001. "On Change V—Riding the Waves of Change: Insights from Transforming Institutions." Paper in an occasional paper series of the American Council on Education Project on Leadership and Institutional Transformation and the Kellogg Forum on Higher Education Transformation. www.acenet.edu/bookstore/pdf/on-change/on-changeV.pdfyes. Download at www.acenet.edu/bookstore/pdf/on-change/on-changeV.pdf.

European Foundation for Quality Management. 2006. EFQM model. Retrieved February 10, 2006. <www.valuebasedmanagement.net/methods_efqm.html>.

Ewell, P. 1994. "Developing Statewide Performance Indicators for Higher Education." In *Charting Higher Education Accountability: A Sourcebook on State-Level Performance Indicators,* edited by S. S. Ruppert. Denver: Education Commission of the States.

Falchikov, N., and D. Boud. 1989. "Student Self-Assessment in Higher Education: A Meta-Analysis." *Review of Educational Research* 59. 395–430.

Farrar, M. 2000. "Structuring Success: A Case Study in the Use of the EFQM Excellence Model in School Improvement." *Total Quality Management* 11(4, 5, and 6): 691–96.

Flynn, B. B., and B. Saladin. 2001. "Further Evidence on the Validity of the Theoretical Models Underlying the Baldrige Criteria." *Journal of Operations Management* 19(6): 617–52.

Franz, R. S. 1998. "Whatever You Do, Don't Treat Your Students Like Customers." *Journal of Management Education* 22(1): 63–69.

Friedman, D., and P. H. Hoffman. 2001. "The Politics of Information: Building a Relational Database to Support Decision-Making at a Public University." *Change* 33(3): 51–57.

Galloway, L. 1998. "Quality Perceptions of Internal and External Customers: A Case Study in Education Administration." *TQM Magazine* 10(1). 20–26.

Garvin, D. A. 1998. "Building a Learning Organization." In *Knowledge Management.* Cambridge, Mass.: Harvard Business School Press.

Gates, S. M., C. H. Augustine, R. Benjamin, T. K. Bikson, T. Kaganoff, D. G. Levy, J. S. Moini, and R. W. Zimmer. 2002. *Ensuring Quality and Productivity in Higher Education: An Analysis of Assessment Practices.* San Francisco: Jossey-Bass.

Gempesaw II, C. M. 2004. "Recruiting and Supporting Academic Leaders at the University of Delaware." In *Pursuing Excellence in Higher Education: Eight Fundamental Challenges,* edited by B. D. Ruben, 309-314. San Francisco: Jossey-Bass.

Ghobadian, A., and J. S. Woo. 1996. "Characteristics, Benefits, and Shortcomings of Four Major Quality Awards." *International Journal of Quality and Reliability Management* 13(2): 10–44.

Gibbs, P. 2001. "Higher Education as a Market. A Problem or Solution?" *Studies in Higher Education* 26(1): 85–94.

Giber, D., L. Carter, and M. Goldsmith. 2000. *Best Practices in Leadership Development Handbook*. San Francisco: Jossey-Bass.

Gmelch, W. H. 2000. "Leadership Succession: How New Deans Take Charge and Learn the Job." *Journal of Leadership Studies* 7(30): 68–87.

Gmelch, W. H., and V. D. Miskin. 1995. *Chairing an Academic Department*. Thousand Oaks, Calif.: Sage.

Goleman, D. 1998. "What Makes a Leader?" *Harvard Business Review* 76(6): 92–102.

Grant, D., E. Mergen, and S. Widrick. 2004. "A Comparative Analysis of Quality Management in U.S. and International Universities." *Total Quality Management and Business Excellence* 15(4): 423–38.

Graves, S. B. 1995. "Common Principles of Quality Management and Development Economics." *Quality Management Journal* 2(2): 65–79.

Hansen, M. T., N. Nohria, and T. Tierney. 1999. "What's Your Strategy for Managing Knowledge?" *Harvard Business Review*, March–April, pp. 106–16.

Hecht, I. W. D. 2006. "Becoming a Department Chair: To Be or Not to Be." *Effective Practices for Academic Leaders* 1(3): 1–16.

Heifetz, R. A. 1994. *Leadership without Easy Answers*. Cambridge, Mass.: Harvard University Press.

Hexter, E. S. 1997. *Case Studies in Strategic Performance Measurement*. New York: The Conference Board.

Hill, Y., L. Lomas, and J. MacGregor. 2003. "Students' Perceptions of Quality in Higher Education." *Quality Assurance in Education* 11(1): 15–20.

Horsburgh, M. 1999. "Quality Monitoring in Higher Education: The Impact on Student Learning." *Quality in Higher Education* 5(1): 9–25.

Huisman, J., and J. Currie. 2004. "Accountability in Higher Education: Bridge over Troubled Water?" *Higher Education* 48(4): 529–51.

Jack, E. P., P. R. Stephens, and J. R. Evans. 2001. "An Integrative Summary of Doctoral Research in Quality Management." *Production and Operations Management* 10: 363–82.

Jackson, N., and H. S. Lund. 2000. *Benchmarking for Higher Education*. Buckingham, U.K.: Society for Research into Higher Education and Open University Press.

Jacob, R. 2004. "An Empirical Assessment of the Financial Performance of Malcolm Baldrige Award Winners." *International Journal of Quality and Reliability Management* 21(8): 897.

Jasinski, J. 2004. "Strategic Planning via Baldrige: Lessons Learned." *New Directions for Institutional Research*, no. 123: 27.

Jenkins, L. 2003. *Improving Student Learning: Applying Deming's Quality Principles in the Classroom*. 2nd ed. Milwaukee: American Society for Quality Press.

Johnson, R., and D. Seymour. 1996. "The Baldrige as an Award and Assessment Instrument for Higher Education." In *High Performing Colleges I: Theory and Concepts*, edited by D. Seymour. Maryville, Mo.: Prescott.

Jones, J. E., and W. L. Bearley. 1996. *360° Feedback: Strategies, Tactics, and Techniques for Developing Leaders.* Amherst, Mass.: HRD Press.

Jones, S. 2003. "Measuring the Quality of Higher Education: Linking Teaching Quality Measures at the Delivery Level to Administrative Measures at the University Level." *Quality in Higher Education* 9(3): 223–29.

Joseph, M., and J. Beatriz. 1999. "Customer Perception of Service Quality in Higher Education: Strategic Implications." *Journal of Customer Service in Marketing and Management* 5(4): 17–31.

Joseph, M., and B. Joseph. 1997. "Service Quality in Education: A Students' Perspective." *Quality Assurance in Education* 5(1): 26–37.

Joseph, M., M. Yakhou, and G. Stone. 2005. "An Educational Institution's Quest for Service Quality: Customers' Perspective." *Quality Assurance in Education* 13(1): 66–82.

Kanji, G., A. Malaek, A. Tambi, and W. Wallace. 1999. "A Comparative Study of Quality Practices in Higher Education Institutions in the U.S. and Malaysia." *Total Quality Management* 10(3): 357–71.

Kanji, G., and W. Wallace. 2000. "Business Excellence through Customer Satisfaction." *Total Quality Management* 11(7): 979–98.

Kaplan, R. S., and D. P. Norton. 1992. "The Balanced Scorecard—Measures That Drive Performance." *Harvard Business Review* 70(1): 71–79.

Kaplan, R. S., and D. P. Norton. 1993. "Putting the Balanced Scorecard to Work." *Harvard Business Review* 71(5): 134–47.

Kaplan, R. S., and D. P. Norton. 1996. *The Balanced Scorecard.* Cambridge, Mass.: Harvard Business School.

Kaplan, R. S., and D. P. Norton. 2001. *The Strategy-Focused Organization.* Cambridge, Mass.: Harvard Business School.

Keith, B. 2004 *Contexts for Learning.* Stillwater, Okla.: New Forums Press.

Kellogg Commission. 2001. *Returning to Our Roots: Executive Summaries of the Reports of the Kellogg Commission on the Future of State and Land-Grant Universities.* Washington, D.C.: National Association of State Universities and Land-Grant Colleges. <www.nasulgc.org/Kellogg/kellogg.htm>.

Knight, P. T., and P. R. Trowler. 2001. *Departmental Leadership in Higher Education.* Buckingham, U.K.: Open University Press.

Koch, J. V., and J. L. Fisher. 1998. "Higher Education and Total Quality Management." *Total Quality Management* 9(8): 659–79.

Kotter, J. P. 2001. "What Leaders Really Do." *Harvard Business Review* 79(11): 85–97.

Kotter, J. P., and D. S. Cohen. 2002. *The Heart of Change: Real-Life Stories of How People Change Their Organizations.* 1st ed. Boston: Harvard Business School Press.

Kouzes, J. M, and B. Z. Posner. 1995. *The Leadership Challenge.* San Francisco: Jossey-Bass.

Kuh, G. D. 2001. "Assessing What Really Matters to Student Learning." *Change* 33(3): 10–17, 66.

Lagrosen, S. 1999. "TQM Goes to School: An Effective Way of Improving School Quality." *TQM Magazine* 11(5): 328–32.

Lagrosen, S., R. Seyyed-Hashemi, and M. Leitner. 2004. "Examination of the Dimensions of Quality in Higher Education." *Quality Assurance in Education* 12(2): 61–69.

Lehr, J. K., and R. E. Rice. 2002. "Organizational Measures as a Form of Knowledge Management: A Multi-theoretic, Communication-Based Exploration." *Journal of the American Society for Information Science and Technology* 53(12): 1060–73.

Lehr, J. K., and B. D. Ruben. 1999. "Excellence in Higher Education: A Baldrige-Based Self-Assessment Guide for Higher Education." *Assessment Update* 11(1): 1–4.

Leonard, D. 2002. "The Self-Assessment Matrix: A Baldrige-Based Tool for the Introduction, Training, and Assessment of Organizational Performance Excellence." *Quality Management Forum* 28: 6–9.

Leonard, D. 2003. "Tips for Gaining Maximum Value from Baldrige or State Quality Award Site Visits and Feedback Reports." *Quality Management Forum* 29: 12–13.

Leonard, D., and R. McAdam. 2003. "Impacting Organizational Learning: The Training and Experiences of Quality Award Examiners and Assessors." *Journal of European Industrial Training* 27(1): 16–21.

Leonard, D., and M. K. Reller. 2004. "Simplify Baldrige for Healthcare." *Quality Progress* 37(9): 35–44.

Light, R. J. 2001. *Making the Most of College: Students Speak Their Minds.* Cambridge, Mass.: Harvard University Press.

Lomas, L. 2004. "Embedding Quality: The Challenges for Higher Education." *Quality Assurance in Education* 12(4): 157–65.

Long, P., T. Tricker, M. Rangecroft, and P. Gilroy. 1999. "Measuring the Satisfaction Gap: Education in the Marketplace." *Total Quality Management* 10(4 and 5): 772–78.

Lundquist, R. 1997. "Quality Systems and ISO 9000 in Higher Education." *Assessment and Evaluation in Higher Education* 22(2): 159–72.

"Managed Environments for Reflective Portfolio-Based Learning." 2005. <www.eportfolios.ac.uk/>.

Massy, W. F. 2003. *Honoring the Trust: Quality and Cost Containment in Higher Education.* Bolton, Mass.: Anker.

Mayer, P. S. 2002. *The Human Side of Knowledge Management: An Annotated Bibliography.* Greensboro, N.C.: Center for Creative Leadership Press.

McAdam, R. S., and W. R. Welsh. 2000. "A Critical Review of the Business Excellence Quality Model Applied to Further Education Colleges." *Quality Assurance in Education* 8(3): 120–30.

McGovern, D., L. Foster, and K. Ward. 2002. "College Leadership: Learning from Experience." *Journal of Leadership Studies* 8(3): 29–41.

McInerney, C. 2002. "Knowledge Management and the Dynamic Nature of Knowledge." *Journal of the American Society for Information Science and Technology* 53(12): 1009–18.

Mergen, E., D. Grant, and S. Widrick. 2000. "Quality Management Applied to Higher Education." *Total Quality Management* 11(3): 345–52.

Middle States Commission on Higher Education. 2002. *Characteristics of Excellence in Higher Education: Eligibility Requirements and Standards for Accreditation.* Philadelphia: Middle States Commission on Higher Education.

Middle States Commission on Higher Education. 2003a. *Resources for Student Learning Assessment.* Philadelphia: Middle States Commission on Higher Education.

Middle States Commission on Higher Education. 2003b. *Student Learning Assessment: Options and Resources.* Philadelphia: Middle States Commission on Higher Education.

Middle States Commission on Higher Education. 2005. *Assessing Student Learning and Institutional Effectiveness: Understanding Middle States Expectations.* Philadelphia: Middle States Commission on Higher Education. <www.msche.org/publications/Assessment_Expectations051222081842.pdf>.

Middle States Commission on Higher Education. 2006. *Characteristics of Excellence in Higher Education: Eligibility Requirements and Standards for Accreditation.* Philadelphia: Middle States Commission on Higher Education.

Miller, C. 2006. "Accountability/Consumer Information." Issue paper 3. Secretary of Education's Commission on the Future of Higher Education. <www.ed.gov/about/bdscomm/list/hiedfuture/reports/miller.pdf>.

Mintzberg, H. 1994. *The Rise and Fall of Strategic Planning.* New York: Macmillan.

Montano, C. B., and G. H. Utter. 1999. "Total Quality Management in Higher Education: An Application of Quality Improvement in a University." *Quality Progress* 32(8): 52–59.

Morley, J. E. 2004. "The Business of Higher Education." *In Pursuing Excellence in Higher Education: Eight Fundamental Challenges,* edited by B. D. Ruben, 332-337. San Francisco: Jossey Bass.

National Communication Association. 2006. "Suggested Assessment Techniques and Methods." <www.natcom.org/nca/Template2.asp?bid=282>.

Nelser, M. 2004. "Using the Baldrige Criteria for Institutional Improvement: The Excelsior College Outcomes Assessment Framework." In *Contexts for Learning,* edited by B. Keith, 65–69. Stillwater, Okla.: New Forums Press.

Neumann, A. 1991. "Defining Good Faculty Leadership." *Thought and Action* 7(1): 45–60.

New England Association of Schools and Colleges, Commission on Institutions of Higher Education. 2004. *Draft Standards for Accreditation*. Bedford, Mass.: Commission on Institutions of Higher Education. <www.neasc.org/cihe/revisions/standards_revision.htm>.

Newton, J. 2000. "Feeding the Beast or Improving Quality? Academics' Perceptions of Quality Assurance and Quality Monitoring." *Quality in Higher Education* 6(2): 153–63.

Niven, P. R. 2002. *Balanced Scorecard Step-by-Step: Maximizing Performance and Maintaining Results*. 1st ed. New York: Wiley.

Norman, R. M., Haley, W. J., and A. Haislar. "Applying Excellence in Higher Education in Finance and Administrative Services" In *Pursuing Excellence in Higher Education: Eight Fundamental Challenges*, edited by B. D. Ruben, 190-201. San Francisco: Jossey Bass.

North Central Association of Colleges and Universities. The Higher Learning Commission. 2003. *Institutional Accreditation: An Overview*. Chicago: Commission on Institutions of Higher Education. <www.ncacasi.org/>.

North Central Association of Colleges and Universities. The Higher Learning Commission. 2007. Higher Learning Commission's Academic Quality Improvement Program. <http://AQIP.org>.

Northwest Commission on Colleges and Universities. 2004. *Accreditation Standards*. Redmond, Wash.: Northwest Commission on Colleges and Universities. <www.nwccu.org/Standards%20and%20Policies/Accreditation%20Standards/Accreditation%20Standards.htm>.

O'Neill, M. A., and A. Palmer. 2004. "Importance-Performance Analysis: A Useful Tool for Directing Continuous Quality Improvement in Higher Education." *Quality Assurance in Education* 12(1): 39–52.

Outcalt, C. L., S. K. Faris, and K. N. McMahon, eds. 2001. *Developing Non-Hierarchical Leadership on Campus: Case Studies and Best Practices in Higher Education*. Greenwood Educators' Reference Collection.

Palomba, C. A., and T. W. Banta. 1999. *Assessment Essentials: Planning, Implementing, and Improving Assessment in Higher Education*. San Francisco: Jossey-Bass.

Palomba, C. A., and T. W. Banta. 2001. *Assessing Student Competence in Accredited Disciplines: Pioneering Approaches to Assessment in Higher Education*. Herndon, Va.: Stylus.

Paris, K. A. 1997. "Strategic Planning in the Framework of a Campus-Wide Vision for the Future." *NCA Quarterly* (spring) .

Peiperl, M. A. 2001. "Getting 360° Feedback Right." *Harvard Business Review* 79(1): 142–47.

Przasnyski, Z., and L. S. Tai. 2002. "Stock Performance of Malcolm Baldrige National Quality Award Winning Companies." *Total Quality Management* 13(4): 475–88.

Qayoumi, M. 2000. *Benchmarking and Organizational Change*. Alexandria, Va.: Association of Higher Education Facilities Officers.

Ramsden, P. 1998. *Learning to Lead in Higher Education*. Florence, Ky.: Routledge, ITPBK Distribution Center.

Rosa, M., P. Saraiva, and H. Diz. 2003. "Excellence in Portuguese Higher Education Institutions." *Total Quality Management and Business Excellence* 14(2): 189–97.

Rowley, J. 1997. "Beyond Service Quality Dimensions in Higher Education and towards a Service Contract." *Quality Assurance in Education* 5(1): 7–14.

Ruben, B. D. 1995a. "The Quality Approach in Higher Education: Context and Concepts for Change." In *Quality in Higher Education,* edited by B. D. Ruben, 1–34. New Brunswick, N.J.: Transaction.

Ruben, B. D., ed. 1995b. *Quality in Higher Education.* New Brunswick, N.J.: Transaction.

Ruben, B. D. 1995c. "What Students Remember: Teaching, Learning, and Human Communication." In *Quality in Higher Education,* edited by B. D. Ruben, 189-199. New Brunswick, N.J.: Transaction.

Ruben, B. D. 2003a. *Excellence in Higher Education, 2003–2004: A Baldrige-Based Guide to Organizational Assessment, Planning, and Improvement.* Washington, D.C.: National Association of College and University Business Officers.

Ruben, B. D. 2003b. *Excellence in Higher Education, 2003–2004: Workbook.* Washington, D.C.: National Association of College and University Business Officers.

Ruben, B. D. 2003c. *Excellence in Higher Education, 2003–2004: Facilitator's Guide.* Washington, D.C.: National Association of College and University Business Officers.

Ruben, B. D. 2004. *Pursuing Excellence in Higher Education: Eight Fundamental Challenges.* San Francisco: Jossey-Bass.

Ruben, B. D. 2005a. *Excellence in Higher Education: An Integrated Approach to Assessment, Planning, and Improvement in Colleges and Universities.* Washington, D.C.: National Association of College and University Business Officers.

Ruben, B. D. 2005b. *Excellence in Higher Education: Workbook.* Washington, D.C.: National Association of College and University Business Officers.

Ruben, B. D. 2005c. *Excellence in Higher Education: Facilitator's Guide.* Washington, D.C.: National Association of College and University Business Officers.

Ruben, B. D. 2005d. "Linking Accreditation Standards and the Malcolm Baldrige Framework: An Integrated Approach to Continuous Assessment, Planning, and Improvement." Paper presented at the Annual Conference of the Middle States Commission on Higher Education, December, 2005, Baltimore.

Ruben, B. D. 2006a. "Departmental Effectiveness: What Is It? Why Is It Important? How Can It Be Achieved?" *Effective Practices in Academic Leadership* 1(12).

Ruben, B. D. 2006b. *What Leaders Need to Know and Do: A Competency-Based Leadership Scorecard.* Washington, D.C.: National Association of College and University Business Officers.

Ruben, B. D. 2007. "Higher Education Assessment: Linking Accreditation and the Malcolm Baldrige Criteria." *New Directions for Higher Education* 137, Spring: 59–83.

Ruben, B. D., S. Connaughton, K. Immordino, and J. Lopez. 2004. "What Impact Does the Baldrige/Excellence in Higher Education Self-Assessment Process Have on Institutional Effectiveness?" Presented at the National Consortium for Continuous Improvement in Higher Education, July, Milwaukee.

Ruben, B. D., T. Russ, S. M. Smulowitz, and S. L. Connaughton. 2007. "Evaluating the Impact of Organizational Self-Assessment in Higher Education: The Malcolm Baldrige/Excellence in Higher Education Framework." *Leadership and Organizational Development Journal.* 28(3) In press.

Russo, C. W. 2001. "10 Steps to a Baldrige Award Application." *Quality Progress* 34(8): 49–55.

Salem, P. 1999. *Organization Communication and Change.* Cresskill, N.J.: Hampton Press.

Saraiva, P. M., M. J. Rosa, and J. L. D'Orey. 2003. "Applying an Excellence Model to Schools." *Quality Progress* 36(11): 46–51.

Scholtes, P. R. 1997. *The Leader's Handbook: Making Things Happen, Getting Things Done.* 1st ed. Ontario, Canada: McGraw-Hill.

Schray, V. 2006. "Assuring Quality in Higher Education." Issue paper 14. Secretary of Education's Commission on the Future of Higher Education. <www.ed.gov/about/bdscomm/list/hiedfuture/reports/schray2.pdf>.

Senge, P. M. 1990. *The Fifth Discipline.* New York: Doubleday.

Sevier, R. A. 2000. *Strategic Planning in Education.* New York: Council for Advancement and Support of Education.

Seymour, D. T. 1989. *On Q: Causing Quality in Higher Education.* New York: American Council on Education and Macmillan.

Shergold, K., and D. M. Reed. 1996. "Striving for Excellence: How Self-Assessment Using the Business Excellence Model Can Result in Step Improvements in All Areas of Business Activities." *TQM Magazine* 8(6): 48–52.

Shirks, A., W. B. Weeks, and A. Stein. 2002. "Baldrige-Based Quality Awards: Veterans Health Administration's E-year Experience." *Quality Management in Health Care* 10(3): 47–54.

Shupe, D. A. 1999. "Productivity, Quality, and Accountability in Higher Education." *Journal of Continuing Higher Education* 47(1): 2–13.

Smith, R. M. 1997. "Defining Leadership through Followership: Concepts for Approaching Leadership Development." Paper delivered at the 83rd Annual Meeting of the National Communication Association, November 19–23, Chicago.

Sorensen, C. W., and D. Moen. "Winning the Baldrige Natinal Quality Award" In *Pursuing Excellence in Higher Education: Eight Fundamental Challenges,* edited by B. D. Ruben, 202-215, San Francisco: Jossey Bass.

Southern Association of Colleges and Schools, Commission on Colleges. 2007. Accrediting Standards. Decatur, GA.: Commission on Colleges. <www.sacscoc.org/principles.asp>.

Southern Association of Colleges and Schools, Commission on Colleges. 2006. *Principles of Accreditation: Foundations for Quality Enhancement.* <www.sacscoc.org/pdf/2007%20interim%20principles%20complete.pdf>.

Sousa, R., and C. A. Voss. 2002. "Quality Management Revisited: A Reflective Review and Agenda for Future Research." *Journal of Operations Management* 20(1): 91–109.

Spangehl, S. D. 2000. "Aligning Assessment, Academic Quality, and Accreditation." *Assessment and Accountability Forum* 10(2): 10–11, 19.

Spangehl, S. D. 2004. "Talking with Academia about Quality—The North Central Association of Colleges and Schools, Academic Quality Improvement Project." In *Pursuing Excellence in Higher Education: Eight Fundamental Challenges,* edited by B. D. Ruben, 179-189. San Francisco: Jossey-Bass.

Spellings Commission. 2006a. "Final Report Draft." Commission on the Future of Higher Education. <www.ed.gov/about/bdscomm/list/hiedfuture/reports/0809-draft.pdf>.

Spellings Commission. 2006b. A National Dialogue: The Secretary of Education's Commission on the Future of Higher Education. <www.ed.gov/about/bdscomm/list/hiedfuture/index.html>.

Srikanthan, G., and J. F. Dalrymple. 2002. "Developing a Holistic Model for Quality in Higher Education." *Quality in Higher Education* 8(3): 215–25.

Srikanthan, G., and J. F. Dalrymple. 2003. "Developing Alternative Perspectives for Quality in Higher Education." *International Journal of Educational Management* 17(2 and 3): 126–36.

Suskie, L. 2004. *Assessing Student Learning.* Bolton, Mass.: Anker.

Tam, M. 1999. "Managing Chaos Involves Changing Management: Implications for Transforming Higher Education." *Quality in Higher Education* 5(3): 227–33.

Tam, M. 2001. "Measuring Quality and Performance in Higher Education." *Quality in Higher Education* 7(1): 47–54.

Tam, M. 2002. "Measuring the Effect of Higher Education on University Students." *Quality Assurance in Education* 10(4): 223–28.

Tang, K. H., and M. Zairi. 1998. "Benchmarking Quality Implementation in a Service Context: A Comparative Analysis of Financial Services and Institutions of Higher Learning." *Total Quality Management* 9(8): 669–79.

Temponi, C. 2005. "Continuous Improvement Framework: Implications for Academia." *Quality Assurance in Education* 13(1): 17–36.

Tromp, S. A., and B. D. Ruben. 2004. *Strategic Planning in Higher Education: A Leader's Guide.* Washington, D.C.: National Association of College and University Business Officers.

Unseem, M. 1998. *The Leadership Moment.* New York: Random House.

Vaill, P. B. 1998. *Spirited Leading and Learning.* San Francisco: Jossey-Bass.

Van Der Wielw, T., A. Brown, E. Cowan, R. Millen, and D. Whelan. 2000. "Improvement in Organizational Performance and Self-Assessment Practices by Selected American Firms." *Quality Management Journal* 7(4): 8–22.

Vokurka, R., G. Stading, and J. Brazeal. 2000. "A Comparative Analysis of National and Regional Quality Awards." *Quality Progress* 33(8): 41–49.

Vokurka, R. J. 2001. "The Baldrige at 14." *Journal for Quality and Participation* 24(2).

Volkwein, J. F. 2006. "Coping with the Challenges of Assessment on Campus." Paper presented at the Middle States Commission on Higher Education Annual Conference. December, Philadelphia.

Wallace, J. 1999. "The Case for Student as Customer." *Quality Progress* 32(2): 47–51.

Walsh, A., H. Hughes, and D. P. Maddox. 2002. "Total Quality Management Continuous Improvement: Is the Philosophy a Reality?" *Journal of European Industrial Training* 26(6 and 7): 299–307.

Walvoord, B. E. 2004. *Assessment Clear and Simple: A Practical Guide for Institutions, Departments, and General Education.* San Francisco: Jossey-Bass.

Warzynski, C. C., and B. F. Chabot. 2004. "Leadership Development at Cornell University." In *Pursuing Excellence in Higher Education: Eight Fundamental Challenges,* edited by B. D. Ruben, 315-323. San Francisco: Jossey Bass.

Weinstein, L. A. 1993. *Moving a Battleship with Your Bare Hands.* Madison, Wis.: Magna.

Welsh, J. F., and S. Dey. 2002. "Quality Measurement and Quality Assurance in Higher Education." *Quality Assurance in Education* 10(1): 17–25.

Wenger, E. C., and W. M. Snyder. 2000. "Communities of Practice: The Organizational Frontier." *Harvard Business Review,* January–February, pp. 139–45.

Western Association of Schools and Colleges, Accrediting Commission for Senior Colleges and Universities. 2001. Handbook of Accreditation. Alameda, Calif.: WASC. <www.wascsenior.org/wasc/Doc_Lib/2001%20Handbook.pdf>.

Western Association of Schools and Colleges, Accrediting Commission for Senior Colleges and Universities. 2002. *A Guide to Using Evidence in the Accreditation Process: A Resource to Support Institutions and Evaluation Teams.* Alameda, Calif.: WASC. <www.wascweb.org>.

Willits, B. S., and L. E. Pollack. 2004. "Penn State's Excellence in Leadership and Management Program." In *Pursuing Excellence in Higher Education: Eight Fundamental Challenges,* edited by B. D. Ruben, 324-331. San Francisco: Jossey Bass.

Wolverton, M., and W. H. Gmelch. 2002. *College Deans: Leading from Within.* Westport, Conn.: American Council on Education and Oryz Press.